ALL SAINTS

ALL SAINTS

THE SURPRISING STORY *of* HOW REFUGEES *from* BURMA BROUGHT LIFE TO A DYING CHURCH

MICHAEL SPURLOCK *and* JEANETTE WINDLE

BETHANYHOUSE
a division of Baker Publishing Group
Minneapolis, Minnesota

Published by Bethany House Publishers
11400 Hampshire Avenue South
Bloomington, Minnesota 55438
www.bethanyhouse.com

Bethany House Publishers is a division of
Baker Publishing Group, Grand Rapids, Michigan

Printed in the United States of America

Library of Congress Cataloging-in-Publication Data
Names: Spurlock, Michael, author.
Title: All Saints : the surprising story of how refugees from Burma brought life to a
    dying church / Michael Spurlock and Jeanette Windle.
Other titles: All Saints (Motion picture)
Description: Special movie edition. | Minneapolis, Minnesota : Bethany House,
    2017.
Identifiers: LCCN 2017014765 | ISBN 9780764230271 (trade paper : alk. paper)
Subjects: LCSH: All Saints Episcopal Church (Smyrna (Rutherford County,
    Tenn.))—History. | Tennessee—Smyrna (Rutherford County)—Church history. |
    Refugees—Burma. | Karen (Southeast Asian people)—Burma—Religion.
Classification: LCC BX5980.S55 S68 2017 | DDC 283/.76857—dc23
LC record available at https://lccn.loc.gov/2017014765

17 18 19 20 21 22 23   7 6 5 4 3 2 1

For my wife
and children

But Jesus answered them,
My Father worketh hitherto,
and I work.

Saint John 5:17

Preface

As I write this, my family and I have just returned from a pilgrimage to the Holy Land. As we visited many of the holy sites in Jerusalem, Bethlehem, Nazareth, and other places, I was more deeply aware of how present Jesus' life seemed to me. Present in the sense of incarnate. The wonder and joy of our faith is that God did not despise the places and times he created, but humbled himself to come among us in time and place and act. It was curious to stand in the Jordan and tell my children that we were at the place, or very near to it, where the heavens were torn open, and the Spirit descended upon Jesus, and God's voice was heard from heaven declaring that Jesus was his Son. Or to stand in the place where the Temple stood and recall that when our Lord was presented there as an infant the glory of the Lord filled the Temple as in days of old. Or even to see the stalls of the money changers near the Jerusalem gates and know that in some ways times haven't changed much since Jesus' days. But more than curious, being in those places gave me a sense of well-being that made it difficult to leave. In another time and place, Jesus was there in that same place where I was now, and when he was there he had been about his Father's business.

The story told within the pages of this book is a story I am on intimate terms with because I lived much of it. I will admit that as the converging stories of Ye Win and Father Bu Christ, and many other men and women you will meet within these pages, came to life in the stark witness of words on page, I see that I have lived the most staid and bourgeois portion of this story. My own existential crises seem pitiful in comparison to the life and death struggle my brothers and sisters from Burma have endured. And yet, God used that convergence to his own good purposes.

Some years have passed since the events at the heart of this story. But it still lives within me, even though I have moved on to live in a different city and minister in a different church. It lives within me because it is a living story, and it is ongoing. When I was right in the midst of it I had a difficult time telling it, and as I was often asked, I found it difficult to explain what lessons to take away from it. I have come to know that there are many lessons or insights that can be derived from this narrative, and they keep revealing themselves to me like a spring that wells up from within, refreshing my understanding of what I experienced while vicar of my small, but growing, Tennessee parish.

Despite my difficulty explaining it or teaching from it, even when I was in the midst of the events, they resonated with me because the events were so familiar to me. They were familiar because they lived like the Bible reads. It was easy to recognize God's hand at work in our midst because God is as constant as our needs are constant. At certain points in this story we needed water. How many times in Scripture have I read about God providing water to his people when they were in desperate need of it? So when we were in desperate need, and water appeared in unexpected ways from unexpected sources, we could readily say, "Ah, God is here doing what God has always done." At certain times we needed a particular kind of human giftedness, and God sent us just the right man or woman to fulfill our need, and to help fulfill their sense of vocation. How many times in Scripture do a people in need receive a messenger that brings them the word or gift or skill just right for the moment?

At one point we confronted such a dearth of resources, we thought we might as well light a small fire, prepare our last meal, and lie down and die, yet God caused our meager provision to last far beyond our calculations. Indeed, those meager resources still endure even to the present, and they have always proved sufficient to the needs at All Saints, Smyrna. Our living echoed the lives of other men and women recorded in the Bible and provided comfort and encouragement to those of us living under God's very present providence. Our story, though new and alive to us, is part of the old, old, but ongoing story of God's life and work here on earth. We were living it during the events recorded within these pages, and we are still living it.

In a world where our fellows often ask, "Where is God? Is he real? Does he notice? Does he care?" I can attest that he is very real, he does notice, he does care, and he is right here, right now, alive and well and very much about his business. There was no reason for All Saints to have survived, much less thrived, after it imploded because of human pride and willfulness. If there is no God, what would it matter anyway? But there is one, and only one, and he was in our midst binding up the wounds, commanding us to take up our mats and walk, and leading us through valley and shadow into a place of light, peace, purpose, work, and resurrected life. Why? Because that is what God does for people who long for him, love what he commands, and submit to being led and transformed by him.

What you will find here is a story about a living God, speaking, calling, and seeking to relate to ordinary men and women. You will also find ordinary men and women speaking to God, crying out to him, hearing him, and then trying to live out what they were hearing God ask them to do. You will read about people relating to one another and to God as if it really does matter. What resulted from those relationships is miraculous, but also familiar, and ordinary. Ordinary in the sense that God has always lived, breathed, and moved in these ways. To me, that is a great comfort. God is alive, well, and still at work in his creation and with his people.

"But Jesus answered them, 'My Father is working still, and I am working'" (John 5:17 RSV).

The Reverend Michael Spurlock
Lent 2017

Prologue

The smell was among the worst elements of this never-ending war, even for a battle-hardened soldier like nineteen-year-old Ye Win. The beauty over which he stood guard made the contrast even more stark. Those who compared southeastern Myanmar's hill country to the biblical garden of Eden were not far off. Flowering trees and orchids in yellows, oranges, pinks dotted the scrub jungle. Crystal-clear streams and waterfalls fed mountain folds and valleys, where villages of thatch and bamboo nestled among food crops, fruit trees, and banana palms. Massive teak trees and other hardwoods raised emerald umbrellas to the heavens.

But now the floating mists of a cloud forest served only to provide cover to Burmese troops inching their way uphill. Constant gunfire had frightened off the chitter of monkeys and harsh calls of jungle peafowl and parrots. And the odor! No more the smell of cool damp and crushed vegetation, but of rotting bodies, spent gunpowder, and burning homes.

The odor caught in Ye Win's sinuses, coated his lungs until it seemed he could no longer remember any other scent. Just as he could no longer remember a time before the fighting and killing. Before lying hungry and thirsty on the mountainside in the hope that one more nightfall would hold the Burmese soldiers from further advance.

This particular skirmish had been going on for three days. Like the rest of his unit, Ye Win had been ordered to dig a foxhole into the mortar-loosened soil of the mountain slope, from which vantage the small guerrilla force could harry government troops attempting to capture the mountain village that served as the Karen National Liberation Army's (KNLA) regional command post. But now dusk had fallen, locking both sides into their current positions, since the pitch black of scrub jungle under a rain-cloaked night sky made any movement suicidal.

By now Ye Win had had enough of the foxhole. The loose soil might be an asset when digging a hole, but all day he'd had to keep one eye out for the enemy while bailing out dirt and pebbles that spilled down on his head. Attempting to sleep down here would be futile. Fortunately, a tall patch of bamboo stood only a short belly-crawl from his foxhole. Nightfall covered his hasty scramble. Now he'd stretch out for just a few hours' sleep, returning to his foxhole in ample time before fighting renewed at dawn.

But Ye Win slept longer than he'd intended. He was awakened by the deep bark of a large artillery gun no more than fifty meters away—and by pain. Just what was wrong he realized only when he heard the rain-patter of machine-gun fire striking the bamboo on all sides of his hiding place. Then he saw the blood. He'd been hit in the leg. No, the abdomen. No, both!

"I've been shot! I've been shot!" Ye Win screamed out.

Around him, KNLA resistance forces were driving the Burmese battalion back down the mountainside. Once the enemy had retreated far enough to permit the deploying of stretcher crews, Ye Win was carried back to the KNLA outpost. Triage divulged that Ye Win had, in fact, received three bullet wounds. A field medic administered morphine and removed the bullets. At least temporarily, the fighting was over for Ye Win.

Over the following days, then weeks, Ye Win lay in the crude thatched shelter—the meager outpost field hospital. With no antibiotics available, infection set in, then malaria. Was he going to die? Ye Win faced the possibility squarely. If he died, what would be his eternal destiny?

Ye Win did not doubt there was a God in heaven who watched Ye Win's every move and ultimately controlled his destiny. A majority of the Karen people, Myanmar's largest ethnic minority, remained animist by religion or had converted to the Buddhism of their Burmese conquerors. But Ye Win's own family was among a sizeable percentage who could trace their Christian heritage back four generations to Adoniram Judson and other foreign missionaries who'd first brought the gospel of Jesus Christ to the Karen, Kachin, Lisu, and other hill peoples of Burma, as Myanmar had once been called. Ye Win's father was a seminary graduate and pastor. Two of his older siblings were evangelists.

But Ye Win himself had turned his back on that life when he'd first joined the Karen resistance army at age thirteen. He couldn't remember the last time he'd set foot in a church. His world, his heart had been so filled with hate, with killing. How could he call out to God with so much blood on his hands?

By the end of three weeks, it had become clear that Ye Win was not healing. That was when his commanding officer came by with new orders. The refugee camps across the Burmese border in Thailand had better medical care available. Their own command post was now overrun with refugees burned out of their homes during the most recent skirmish with government troops. Ye Win's assignment was to guide these refugees across the border into Thailand and remain there to seek medical attention for his own festering wounds.

The distance was less than fifty kilometers. But reaching the refugee camps necessitated maneuvering through Burmese army lines, navigating dense jungle, and crossing a river. Ye Win himself was weak from unhealed wounds, while the refugees included women, small children, and the elderly, many of them sick, starving, or weak from malnutrition, so the trek took three full days. When outlying scouts alerted Ye Win by Walkie-Talkie that Burmese troops were approaching, the group would dig into the thick underbrush, freezing in place until the all clear was given. Even small children and babies learned quickly to maintain complete silence.

At night the group huddled together in the jungle, unable even to light a fire for cooking and safety, since their human enemy was a far greater threat than leopards, pythons, venomous snakes, and other predators. By the third day, all food and water was gone. Land mines were another constant danger.

At last they reached the Salween River that marked the border between Myanmar and Thailand. Canoes were waiting to ferry them across the river to a small refugee camp that catered mostly to displaced Karen. Only after delivering his charges to safety did Ye Win himself collapse. The camp clinic administered antibiotics and malaria medicine, but for more than a day, Ye Win lay unconscious.

By the third day, the malarial fever was gone, but Ye Win remained too weak to walk. The only available food was rice, with no protein to help him recover strength. Contaminated water left him with giardia, a parasite that causes extreme diarrhea. Even worse, he felt completely alone. Friends who'd been sent here to recuperate from their own battle wounds had either returned to the front lines or died. The death rate was, in fact, so high that bodies were simply dumped into the river and left to float out to sea.

By this point, Ye Win was certain he would die. Not that he felt any real desire to keep living. Now that the constant fighting, running, and hiding was over, he had nothing to occupy his time or his mind. As he lay sleepless on his thin mat, his thoughts drifted to the God his parents and grandparents and great-grandparents had worshiped. The God he had once prayed to in simple faith as a child. Thoughts became prayers.

But Ye Win did not pray for healing or even to live. Instead he prayed, *God, I am so tired of fighting. I am so tired of killing. I have seen so many people dying. I want to start walking with you. If you will make it possible for me to stop fighting, to stop killing, I will serve you with the rest of my life.*

Little did Ye Win know how soon God would answer that prayer or how far from home it would take him. Or how many lives would be impacted by his simple commitment to God.

1

Would today be his last time to walk this aisle? To preach God's Word or serve the Eucharist of Christ in this sanctuary? Father Michael Spurlock took his place in the procession wending down the center aisle, his own green-and-gold vestments contrasting with the white surplices of the acolytes and lay servers.

All Saints Episcopal Church in Smyrna, Tennessee, was not a large structure. But its steeply slanted gray roof and rustic redbrick exterior topped by a Celtic cross had captured Michael's heart at first glimpse. Completing its resemblance to some English or Scottish village church was its location atop a green hillock, commanding a glorious view of fertile countryside, thick with trees and threaded by a creek.

Indoors, the cherry-stained beams of a soaring ceiling contrasted with the simplicity of white walls, clear glass windows, and plain wooden pews. Above the altar at the front was an eighteenth-century Belgian painting of Christ on the cross with Adam's skull at its base, a reminder that "as by one man's disobedience many were made sinners, so by the obedience of one [Christ] shall many be made righteous" (Romans 5:19). Opposite it at the rear of the sanctuary, a round stained-glass window depicted the Lamb of God triumphant from Revelation, chapter 5.

But Father Michael's favorite detail was the stained-glass window in the fellowship hall, a depiction of St. Polycarp, first-century bishop of the original Smyrna in Asia Minor. Its border was inscribed with Polycarp's courageous response when ordered to recant his faith or be burned at the stake: "Eighty-six years have I served him [Jesus], and he has done me no wrong. How can I blaspheme my King and my Savior?"

It was not just the serene loveliness of this place he'd miss. This was his church, his congregation, and Father Michael Spurlock was beginning to realize just how much he wanted to stay. But the emptiness of the pews as the procession threaded past, a sparse scattering of worshipers across the front as Michael turned to face the congregation, were a reminder of the stark reality. Sure, there were more faces than when he'd preached his first sermon here only nine months prior. Perhaps there were forty in attendance this morning instead of twenty-five. But not nearly enough to maintain a church infrastructure, much less pay a vicar's salary. Especially with the additional burden of an $850,000 mortgage with a monthly interest-only payment of $5,500. Hardly an easy assignment for any seminary graduate's first parish.

But Michael had been forewarned. Once among the fastest-growing congregations in the Tennessee diocese, All Saints was a relatively new parish, the result of an intentional church-planting effort by the diocese. Its beginning had been a Bible study meeting in a storefront. The church had been incorporated in 1997, this beautiful building consecrated in 2001.

But just months before Michael's arrival, All Saints had undergone a major split. Most of the congregation had left, along with bank accounts, furnishings, even the vestments, chalices, and other communion ware. The wrongs of the split itself were not pertinent to Michael's mission. In fact, the tiny remaining congregation he'd inherited was as divided in opinion as those who'd left. But what those who'd stayed did agree on was that All Saints was their church, schism was not the way to solve their problems, and they simply were not leaving.

Michael remembered all too well when Bishop Bauerschmidt, newly appointed to oversee this diocese, had presented him with this assignment. With such a small remaining congregation and huge debt, options seemed limited. Logic dictated closing down the church, selling the property to pay off the mortgage, then beginning again elsewhere. But both the bishop and Michael were reluctant to see any church close its doors.

"Just go down and be a good priest to them," Bishop Bauerschmidt had advised.

Michael had not said yes immediately. Stepping into a deeply broken church with no practical pastoral experience and as its only full-time paid staff was not what he'd anticipated upon graduating from seminary. It seemed to be a place filled with spiritual land mines and needing an experienced hand to take over. And he had a wife to consider, along with a newborn daughter and seven-year-old son. Aimee had already carried a heavy load, working multiple jobs and caring for their son, Atticus, during three years of seminary. Not to mention the new baby. Was it fair to her even to consider such a difficult assignment?

Michael also couldn't forget the reaction of Karl Burns, his best friend from seminary, when Karl had heard the news. "Wow!" he'd exclaimed. "If you turn that place around, you'll be a hero. But if you don't, no one will blame you, because that's impossible!"

When confronted with the assignment from his bishop, Michael had asked, "What if I don't accept the position in Smyrna? What are my other options?"

"I don't know," the bishop had responded, "but I want you to at least go down and take a look."

That Michael could do. The church had been locked and empty when he finally arrived at All Saints. But when he'd stood on that green knoll, looking out over the fields, creek, and trees that made up twenty-two acres of church property, when he'd peeked through the arched glass window into the simple sanctuary, he'd felt a deep peace and happiness. God was indeed calling him to this place. This was his new home. With God's help, he would seek to bring healing to this congregation. And somehow, if God willed, he'd find a way to keep the doors of All Saints open.

Nine months later, no such way had come to light. The church had experienced some modest growth in numbers, but they needed to triple in attendance and giving just to break even. Far more so to cover Michael's own stipend, currently a mission project of the diocese.

By late fall, the church council had reluctantly agreed that putting the All Saints property up for sale was their only option. Each Sunday since, Michael and his congregation had wondered whether or not they would still be worshiping in their building the next month. But one delay after another had allowed Michael to celebrate his first Christmas as vicar at All Saints. Then came further setbacks, and before they knew it Michael was celebrating his first Easter there as well.

But now the delays appeared to be over. An interested party was prepared to make an offer for All Saints. The bishop's council had approved the sale of the property and was prepared to accept the offer. If they did accept, the congregation's last days worshiping in their building would come soon. Michael refused to consider that this might be the end. A church was not its building, after all, but its people. They'd started once as a small group studying the Bible in a storefront. If necessary, they could start again.

If we are to grow, we will need a purpose greater than building maintenance. It was not the first time the concern had crossed Michael's mind. *We can't ask people to attend just so we can meet our debt or pay my salary or even to help us build a new building. We need to heal as a congregation. But we also need to discern the mission to which God has called us here in Smyrna.*

The procession had now reached the front of the sanctuary, the last notes of the opening hymn fading away. Turning to the congregation for the opening acclamation from *The Book of Common Prayer*, Michael noticed the visitors immediately. Not just because he had the faces of his own small flock well memorized. The three newcomers—two men and a woman—sitting in the rear of the sanctuary were most definitely not locals. Their bronze features and black hair, the men's intricately woven and tasseled vests, and the woman's brightly embroidered blouse and skirt caused Michael to wonder whether they were of Aztec, Mayan, Native American, or even of Southeast Asian descent.

Other than the pleasure of seeing newcomers in church, Michael thought little more of the visitors as he continued through the rest of the service. After the closing organ voluntary, he returned to his office to change out of his vestments as was customary. He'd already seen his wife heading over to the newcomers, so he didn't need to worry about whether they were being made to feel welcome. A petite brunette, Aimee had an outgoing, warm personality that made every new acquaintance feel at home.

A knock came at the office door and his wife poked her head in. "You have some guests here who'd like to speak to you."

The newcomers followed Aimee into the office. As was typical, she'd already learned their names. "This is John and Daisy Kunoo," she introduced, signaling an older couple. She then indicated a strongly built younger man in his late twenties or early thirties. "And this is their son, Ye Win. They are Karen, recent immigrants to the Smyrna area. And they have a question they'd like to ask about our church."

"Korean?" Michael repeated. So his guess of Southeast Asia was correct.

"No, not Korean." Aimee quickly set him straight. "*Karen.* From Myanmar. What they used to call Burma. And they're Christians. From the Episcopal Church there, can you believe it? Or Anglican, I guess they'd call it. Ye Win speaks English, so I'll let him explain."

2

Ye Win was studying the Anglo pastor seated on the opposite side of the table as closely as the older man was examining his three visitors. Father Michael looked welcoming enough, if uncertain. But how to explain the Kunoo family history in one brief encounter? It was confusing enough to Ye Win, and he'd lived with it his entire life. But he began to speak, slowly, translating in his mind to this man's language and forming the difficult sounds with care.

The Kunoo clan was famous—or infamous, depending on one's point of view—among the Karen tribal group of southeast Burma and western Thailand for two things. First, they were Christians. In the 1920s, Ye Win's grandfather, Saw Kunoo, became the first in his village to convert to Christianity, at which point he took a biblical first name, Joseph. His descendants still tell the story of how family members ostracized Joseph for his Christian faith.

Already married, Joseph had two young sons who became gravely ill when an influenza epidemic swept through the village. His wife had become a Christian as well, and Joseph's parents were convinced spirits were attacking their grandsons because the couple had abandoned the tribe's traditional animistic religion. His mother would not even approach their home, but shouted from a distance that the village shaman had told her the boys were sick because their parents had become Christians.

"If you don't come back to our own religion, my grandsons will die," she called. "If they die, I will come and kill both of you."

With no doctor or medicine available, Joseph and his wife simply dedicated themselves to prayer. By now many in the village had died. But a few days later, Joseph's mother noticed her two grandsons playing outside, alive and well.

"Look, this is Christianity!" she called out. "Our spirits aren't strong like this Christian religion."

Within a short time, most of Joseph Kunoo's extended family had become Christians, as had other families among the surrounding villages. There were reasons why the Karen, above many other people groups in Burma, were drawn to Christianity. Their own tribal legends centered around an all-powerful God called Y'Wa, who like the biblical Yahweh had created the world and placed the first man and woman in a beautiful garden. There the man and woman ate forbidden fruit, bringing sin and death into the world. Like Lucifer, Naw K'Paw, the Karen version of mankind's corruptor and tempter, had once served Y'Wa but had been cast from Y'Wa's presence for disobedience. Karen legends even spoke of a holy book that had been taken from the Karen and would one day be returned, leading the Karen to a better future and freedom.

Some Karen Christians today believe these legends indicate the Karen were actual descendants of one of the ten lost tribes of Israel. Other scholars believe the Karen must have had contact with early Christian communities in their nomadic wanderings before arriving in Southeast Asia, though a lack of any references to the life, death, or resurrection of Jesus Christ make this less probable. Another theory is that Karen legends actually predate Israel since they include both a global deluge and a division of languages after the building of a great tower, but no stories reminiscent of Israel's own turbulent history.

Whatever the historical truth, when British and American missionaries brought the gospel to Burma in the early 1800s, the similarities to their own legends encouraged many Karen to embrace Christianity as a direct message from Y'Wa and the Bible as their lost holy book returned to them at last. Baptist, Anglican, and Catholic churches soon competed with Buddhist temples and the occasional Muslim mosque in major cities as well as rural villages and towns.

Burma had been part of the British Empire since it was annexed as part of British India in 1853. In 1886, its monarchy was abolished and replaced with a British governor. By this time, a sizeable percentage of the Karen people, along with the Kachin, Shin, and other hill country tribal groups, were not only staunch Christians but also loyal allies of the British. Fierce fighters, they served as jungle guides and soldiers for the British in the Anglo-Burmese wars of 1826, 1852, and 1886, as well as during World War I.

There was plenty of historic and political rationale for this. The Karen people had no reason to love the Burmese, who had conquered their homeland and driven them into the hills. The Burmese were also Buddhists, and persecution of Karen Christian converts had been persistent, including such torture as crucifixion, burning of Christian homes and churches, as well as imprisoning converts. Under British rule, Karen and other Christians worshiped freely.

From the Burmese point of view, rightly or wrongly, it was felt that the British favored Christian converts, giving them far greater representation in the military and colonial administration than Buddhists, all of which came to a head during World War II.

Much has been told of British and Indian forces fighting bravely in the Burmese jungles to prevent the Japanese from sweeping west across British India. The Karen remember well their own contribution. By the end of World War II, at least 50,000 Karen troops were serving with the allies. Their knowledge of the local terrain and jungle warfare made possible the success of guerrilla operations against the Japanese. When British forces were driven from Burma in 1942, it was the Karen who covered the British retreat and helped them escape safely from the Japanese.

Meanwhile, the Burmese had thrown their lot in wholeheartedly with the Japanese. Burmese military leaders, including those who would become the post-independence ruling junta, traveled to

Japan to learn military tactics and pledge allegiance. They organized the Burma Independence Army (BIA) to fight on behalf of the Japanese. The BIA razed countless Karen villages to the ground while thousands of Karen, from fighting soldiers down to the smallest child, were slaughtered for their support of the British.

Christians were singled out by the Japanese as well as Burmese troops. In Joseph Kunoo's village, neighbors begged the Kunoo family to post some Buddhist symbol on their house. They had heard that the Japanese were coming to kill the village's most notorious Christian family. Joseph answered courageously, "No, I won't betray my Lord."

One of Joseph's brothers, who lived with his family some distance away, had also been identified to the Japanese as a leader of the small Christian church in his village. The two families decided that if the Japanese were going to kill them, they might as well die together rather than separately, so Joseph's family traveled to his brother's village. As word came that Japanese troops were approaching, the Kunoo family and other Christians gathered in the small church compound and began to pray. They had already heard of Christian families martyred in nearby villages and were prepared for the worst.

When the Japanese force arrived, a young man who was the village chief emerged to greet them. Pulling out his sword, the Japanese commander demanded, "Where are the Christians? This knife is thirsting for Christian blood."

Though not a convert himself, the chief had nothing against his Christian neighbors. Still, his subsequent actions took great courage. Ingratiatingly, he invited the Japanese to rest from their travels while the villagers prepared them a meal.

"Don't worry about the Christians. They won't run away," he told the Japanese commander, adding with a snicker, "And they are easy to kill. When they pray, they already have their heads bowed, so you can just cut their heads off!"

The chief then called for a pig to be butchered and a barbecue prepared, meanwhile bringing out ample alcohol for the thirsty

Japanese troops. By the time the troops had finished feasting, it was getting late. The Japanese commander didn't want to be caught on the mountainside after dark, so he called for the village chief. "We must leave, so we need to kill the Christians now."

"Don't worry," the chief reassured the commander, "I personally will be responsible for killing them. You go now, before it is too dark for you to travel."

"Just make sure to kill them all," the Japanese commander ordered. After another round of alcohol, he led his troops down the mountain. The chief hurried to the church to let the Christians know they were safe. The Japanese never did return, and soon afterward, that young village chief became a Christian. Years later, when Ye Win's uncle Ga Nel Me, a small child at this time, was a university student, he had the privilege of sitting in a chapel assembly while the man who had saved their family shared his testimony of faith.

Yet the struggle for self-rule and human rights between the Karen—along with other hill tribes—and the Burmese military regime was well on its way to becoming the longest civil war in modern history. Ye Win's father, John Kunoo, born in 1943, and John's younger brother, Ga Nel Me, born in 1945, the seventh and eighth born of Joseph's now large family, remember every year of that conflict.

※ ※ ※

It would be months, even years, before Father Michael Spurlock learned the Kunoo story in its entirety—much less that of the Karen, a people group he admitted he didn't even know existed. Though it was not yet clear what brought this trio to Smyrna, much less to All Saints, Michael had been able to follow the younger man's strongly accented synopsis enough to grasp the most important issues. These three visitors were strangers in a strange land. And they were Michael Spurlock's own brothers and sisters in Christ.

"So how can I help you?" Michael asked courteously. "My wife mentioned you had a question you wanted to ask?"

The younger man appeared to be the only one fluent in English, since he again answered for the group. Ye Win was his name, Michael reminded himself. But his query was not one Michael had expected.

"We want to know if your church believes in Jesus."

"Yes, of course we do!" Michael responded, somewhat stunned. What could have elicited such a question about any Christian church?

The young man demonstrated visible relief. "We were told that you did not, so this is good. Would it be possible then to schedule a meeting to speak with you? As we explained to your wife, we are searching for a church that we might attend here in this country. In our own country, we were Anglican, and we were told there that Anglican churches in the United States are called Episcopalian. So we came here, but we were warned that you did not believe in Jesus or God's Word as we do, so we wanted to find out first."

Clearly there was more to this story. Who would have told these people such a thing about All Saints? Was it a disgruntled former member from the splitting faction? Whoever it was, had they truly believed this falsehood, or was it deliberate malice? Not that it really mattered now.

"Absolutely, we believe in Jesus Christ as our Lord and Savior," Michael stated firmly. "We have staked our lives on his saving power. We believe that he died for our sins and rose again. We believe in the Bible as the Word of God. As to attending All Saints"—Michael looked from Ye Win to his parents—"you are, of course, welcome. Is this all of your family?"

"Oh, no, there is more of our family." Ye Win gave a quick negative shake of the head. "But it is not only our family that is seeking a church. It is our entire community—perhaps seventy or more."

3

Seventy-plus! That was almost twice All Saints' current attendance. Father Michael, the entire church, in fact, had been praying fervently for new members to swell their ranks. But this was hardly what any of them had envisioned.

Any doubts about how serious his three visitors had been were dispelled the next Sunday when a large, battered van, Ye Win behind the wheel, discharged a number of Karen passengers, far more than any vehicle could have provided with legal seat restraints, onto the grassy front lawn. By the time the worship service began, Ye Win had made two more round trips. Other Karen were pouring in off the highway on foot or riding bicycles. How far had they come? Would any of All Saints' Anglo congregation have made it to church that morning without a car?

Three strangers had drawn curiosity from All Saints' small Caucasian congregation. But now there were seventy-plus. And there was no ignoring this bunch. The adults were exotic enough, the women in colorful embroidered blouses and wraparound skirts, the men wearing tasseled vests, hand-tied up the sides and back, over ordinary Walmart shirts and slacks. But taking off their shoes to enter the sanctuary barefoot? And did the men among them not recognize the irreverence of failing to remove their hats before sitting down?

At least these first two groups were relatively quiet and orderly. They even carried what were evidently Bibles and *The Book of*

Common Prayer, though in a strange circular script. Signs of wear made clear these were put to regular use. It was their children who projected the impression of a traveling circus. They were everywhere, running, shouting, climbing on pews, touching the meticulously polished brass and wood of the altar railing. They settled down only fractionally for the processional and liturgy of the morning worship service.

In time, Father Michael would learn that this morning's visitors were accustomed to worshiping in simple bamboo structures with thatch or tin roofs, where congregants crowded close on spread-out mats, a packed-earth courtyard provided ample nursery care for running children, and no shiny or strange furnishings offered distraction. And in time, those same visitors would learn that American congregations kept their shoes on and hats off. Their children too would learn to remain corralled in reasonable quiet and immobility on those long raised wooden benches the people of this strange new land seemed to prefer for seating over a flat, comfortable floor.

But today, Father Michael had never felt less in control of the morning's carefully prepared sacramental rites and liturgy. Blank expressions, a rustle of pages as the visitors attempted to match their unfamiliar script with the announced readings, made clear two-thirds of his congregation had no idea what was being said. Michael could hardly hear his own sermon over the constant murmur of attempted translations—or perhaps just the understandable boredom of incomprehension. And if some of All Saints' small Anglo congregation appeared to be taking the new arrivals in stride, disapproving glances made abundantly clear that others saw only chaos and invasion.

If Michael's own response was far more accepting, it wasn't just for the joy of seeing the church pews full for the first time since he'd arrived at All Saints. He'd spent enough time on Google to have at least a basic grasp of Southeast Asia's more recent history and why these Karen found themselves so far from their homeland. It was a story that compelled compassion and patient understanding from any but the hardest of hearts.

It would take time and painstaking assembly before Michael pieced together Ye Win's own connection to it all, including the second characteristic for which the Kunoo clan was best known.

※ ※ ※

Only when it was clear that the Japanese had lost the war did the Burma Independence Army shift allegiance to the Allies, just in time to claim a seat at the table for peace negotiations. At this point, the British Empire was crumbling all around the globe, one after another of their colonial possessions suing for independence, including British India. The Karen were not worried, since in return for their loyalty and sacrifice, they'd been assured of British support for Karen self-rule in the part of southeast Burma that had been their historic homeland.

So it was with shock and a sense of deep betrayal that the Karen learned of Britain's negotiations with the Burmese to pull out, leaving the BIA military junta de facto rulers of Burma. No provision for autonomy or independence had been made by the British for their most faithful allies, the Karen, or any other of Burma's ethnic minorities, many of whom had also fought for the British.

In January 1948, just six months after the British pulled out of India and Pakistan, Burma declared its independence. Karen and Kachin battalions that had fought the Japanese were merged with the Japanese-trained BIA into a single armed force. In fact, the new army's commander-in-chief was an ethnic Karen, General Smith Dun. But it was an uneasy alliance. The Karen were still agitating for an independent state, while many Burmese hated the Karen for their support of colonial British rule.

Then on Christmas Eve 1948, in what would become a foreshadowing of government policy over the next half century, Burmese troops seized at least eight Karen churches, massacring churchgoers. Over the next month, Burmese troops burned and razed numerous Karen towns and villages, singling out Christian schools and churches as targets. Atrocities included the rape of young Karen girls and the slitting open of pregnant women.

Karen defense forces retaliated. By the end of January 1949, fighting had reached the capital city of Rangoon. Karen general Smith Dun was arrested and replaced by his Burmese deputy, Japanese-trained Ne Win, who over the following decades would preside over one of the longest and most brutal military juntas of modern history.

The Karen in turn organized to protect their people and territory, forming the Karen National Liberation Army (KNLA). Its ranks were filled with well-trained and experienced soldiers who had spent years fighting the Japanese and their BIA allies. Seizing control of significant swatches of Karen territory, they set up their own quasi-government, the Karen National Union (KNU).

So began a civil war that continues to this day, its ever-shifting front lines the long, narrow portion of southeast Burma bordered by the Salween River and neighboring Thailand—specifically, that portion claimed by the Karen people as their ancestral homeland.

This is where the Kunoo clan entered the story. Throughout much of the British Empire, Christian converts had placed a high emphasis on education as well as English language acquisition, which in turn permitted them to advance in the service of Britain's colonial administration. As a result, by the end of World War II, the literacy and education rate was far higher among the Karen and other hill tribes than among ethnic Burmese lowlanders. While Burmese Christians encompassed as many denominations as tribes, thanks to a wide range of Western missionary organizations, the Anglican Church had established a strong presence in Burma since the beginning of British rule in the early nineteenth century. Anglican schools, universities, and hospitals followed.

Among top educational institutions were the Anglican Holy Cross Theological Seminary in Rangoon and St. Peter's Bible School in the Taungoo Diocese, about two hundred kilometers from Rangoon. In a strongly Karen region, St. Peter's was established specifically to train Karen ministry leaders. Even after Ne Win's military coup, foreign missionaries were permitted to teach and evangelize until 1966, when all Western Protestant and Catholic missionaries were expelled from Burma, now renamed Myanmar.

Ye Win's uncle Ga Nel Me had been educated at both St. Peter's and Holy Cross. His plans were to become a church-planting missionary like his father, uncles, and other male clan members. But while Ga Nel Me was studying in Rangoon, the Burmese military launched what they called a "four cut" operation to snuff out rebellious ethnic militias once and for all. The four pillars of its strategy involved wiping out rebel access to food, funds, information, and recruitment.

The strategy was not original. Like other brutal military regimes around the planet, the Ne Win regime had borrowed from Mao Zedong's infamous counter-insurgency tactic: "Drain the sea, and the fish will die." In this case, the Burmese military designated the "sea" as the Karen and other hill tribes. In practice, their "four cut" policy was nothing more than a scorched-earth genocidal assault on ethnic minorities that involved razing villages, slaughtering the inhabitants or rounding them up as slave labor, destroying crops and fruit trees, filling in wells, and poisoning the water, as well as such added atrocities as raping women and young girls.

By now Ga Nel Me was not only studying theology but serving as editor of the Anglican Church theological journal in Rangoon. The news that the Burmese military had burned twenty Karen villages, including his family's own home village, and that his extended family was now one more group of scattered refugees struggling to survive in the jungle, proved the last straw for Ga Nel Me. He became one of many Kunoo clan members who joined the Karen rebel army. So many, in fact, that the Kunoo name became known among both the Karen and Burmese government authorities for its identification with KNLA resistance leadership.

The year was now 1977, and Ga Nel Me was twenty-two years old. He would spend the next twenty years in the jungles and mountains along the Burmese-Thai border as operational commander in the Karen Defense Force as well as personal advisor and secretary to the prime minister of the Karen revolutionary government. His university education and excellent English, acquired in Anglican

Church schools, proved to be unexpectedly valuable combat skills. He also served as a chaplain to Karen Christian forces.

To outsiders, the conjunction of jungle guerrilla fighters and devout Christianity might seem an odd dichotomy. But neither Ga Nel Me nor other Karen Christians saw any incongruity. To the Karen, this was a righteous conflict, a war of self-defense against a godless, brutal regime determined to wipe out their very existence as well as their ethnic and religious identity. And certainly the war was for long intervals a reasonably peaceable stalemate, with the Karen high command building up a prosperous capital in the town of Papun, on the east side of the Yunzalin River no more than thirty kilometers from the Thailand border.

With their emphasis on education, the Karen founded schools, vocational institutes, and clinics within their territory. War orphans came under the care of the Karen National Liberation Army, receiving an education in reading, writing, and math from KNLA-supplied teachers, along with lessons in how to dismantle an AK-47, assemble an improvised explosive device (IED), and apply first aid to a gunshot wound.

But in the end, the stalemate had failed. And as the tide turned, and the Burmese military pushed deeper and deeper into KNLA-held territory, the Karen, like so many of Myanmar's minority ethnic groups, were forced to flee their homes for refugee camps across the border in Thailand or other surrounding nations. It was enough that an entire generation of the Karen diaspora had grown up without having ever seen their homeland, unwanted by the countries in which they'd taken refuge, without a nationality, without rights of citizenship, and without any place on this planet to call their own.

This was the life to which All Saints' newest congregants had been born. The world from which they'd fled to Smyrna, Tennessee.

4

Ye Win had not forgotten Father Michael's promise of a personal meeting. This time he brought along several other men from among the morning's visitors. From their perplexed expressions and quiet murmurs, it was clear that they too understood little of the English being spoken. Ye Win introduced each in turn. Along with his father, John Kunoo, was a stocky man named Christ Paw, whom Michael had noted earlier with a wife and swarm of small children. Christ Paw had been a schoolteacher before being driven out of Myanmar. An older man was introduced as Father Thomas Bu Christ. Michael's ears pricked up to hear that the man was an Anglican priest.

But genuine interest was giving way to dismay as the real reason Ye Win had requested this meeting became clear. The Kunoo family and other Karen were recent arrivals in Smyrna from the Thai refugee camps. Most were Christians, from Anglican, Baptist, and other denominational backgrounds. But they weren't only in need of a church. Few spoke any English or had the skills necessary in this country, such as driving a car. They'd been granted temporary housing assistance but were in dire need of food, clothing, transport, and medical care. Though Michael still knew little about the Karen and even less about what being a refugee entailed, he knew what food, clothing, and other basic necessities added up to for seventy people. And their needs were not just financial, but emotional and spiritual as well.

Michael listened and nodded, but his mind was whirling. He had to admit it: he was afraid! Since he'd arrived at All Saints, he'd set two priorities with the church council and his small congregation. The first had been healing. The small group remaining at All Saints when he'd arrived had been deeply wounded by the breakup of their church. As a congregation, they were facing so many enemies—frustration, anger, despair, betrayal, fear, uncertainty about the future. If All Saints was to have any hope of facing and defeating these enemies, they needed to heal. And to heal, they needed a healer, a physician.

An inexperienced vicar right out of seminary, Michael was well aware he didn't know the first thing about how to address the kind of practical mess All Saints faced. But he did know the only one capable of healing these good people: Jesus Christ. Early on in discussions and planning sessions, meetings and brainstorming, the small remaining group at All Saints had made the commitment to place themselves completely under the authority of Christ.

Eventually, healing had begun to take place in a very noticeable way. Now it was time to move forward with their second priority: mission. Even with the decision to sell all and start over again, there had been a lot of prayer and talk about just how the All Saints congregation could reach beyond their brick walls to find a way and place to serve in Christ's name.

But if their spiritual life was growing stronger, the congregation's material circumstances had not kept pace. And in all their planning and dreaming, taking on a full-scale refugee ministry had not once entered the discussion. The fear that now clutched at Michael's heart was for the members of All Saints. And for the Karen as well. Fear that these refugees, who far outnumbered the original congregation, would overwhelm an already vulnerable church.

After all, All Saints was penniless. Any day, they might be selling their building and moving back to a storefront. And even after the sale, their resources would be modest. How would they even begin helping a people with such deep, deep needs? And there were the obvious cultural and language barriers. How would two such vastly different peoples be able to live with each other? Or even tolerate one another?

And these people weren't ordinary refugees! There were men among them, and maybe even women, who'd been guerrilla soldiers, who'd carried weapons, fought battles, actually killed people. Maybe even some among the group standing in his office. What would his congregation say about inviting in such potential danger and liability? What would his superiors in the diocese say?

Come on, we've got our own problems here! Michael found himself thinking as he listened to Ye Win's earnest plea. His mind flashed back to his seminary friend's statement when he'd accepted the assignment to All Saints. If turning this church around was ranked an impossible task, then certainly no one would blame Michael or the All Saints congregation for taking a pass on this new challenge. Surely there were other larger, thriving, financially stable churches in Smyrna far more capable of taking this on.

But even as those thoughts crossed his mind, even as anxiety and fear and reluctance warred in his heart, Michael was thinking as well about the commitment All Saints had made, the commitment he himself had made, to place Jesus squarely in the center of their community, their daily lives. These visitors were not just inconvenient, needy strangers. They were fellow brothers and sisters in Christ. And Michael knew all too well what it felt like to be searching—not just for a home, a church family, a place to belong, but for a life purpose, an answer to the nameless longing in his own soul.

What would Jesus say to these people were he in Michael's place? What would Jesus do? Pointless questions, since Michael already knew well what Jesus had to say on the matter: "Love your neighbor. . . . Feed my sheep. . . . Love one another . . . as I have loved you. . . . Just as you did it for one of the least of these brothers or sisters of mine, you did for me" (Mark 12:31; John 21:17; 13:34; Matthew 25:40 net).

Brothers or sisters of mine. How could Michael claim to have placed Christ at the center of his life, at the center of his parish ministry, if he was willing to deny with his actions what he had professed with his mouth? After all, just a week earlier, he'd pleaded with God to reveal his purpose for this struggling, small church. To send them a mission.

And suddenly Michael's answer was clear. Looking squarely at Ye Win and his companions, he simply told the truth.

"Look, I don't know how this is going to work out. I don't know how we're going to be of any help to you. As you saw, our congregation is very small. Our building is up for sale, and we don't even know if we will have a place to worship next Sunday. We don't have a lot of resources to help your community. But you are welcome here. All of you. You come on and join us, and we'll all figure it out together."

5

ropping off his companions, Ye Win drove his battered van back to Chalet Apartments, a misnomer for the run-down low-income apartment complex where much of the Karen refugee community in Smyrna lived. His interview with the Anglo vicar had proved worthwhile. Unfortunately, the Karen needed far more than a church to attend on Sundays, and while All Saints had brought back agreeable memories of Anglican Church services back in Myanmar, the vicar's good will alone would not meet the countless varied needs of the Karen.

Ye Win was tired. He'd had to rise by five a.m. (which was not unusual) to ferry all the Karen needing rides to All Saints by service time. Between working a night shift and helping the Karen during the day, Ye Win rarely slept more than four hours a night. And having the only vehicle among the Karen was as much a disadvantage as advantage, since he also had to make rounds mornings and evenings to drive Karen workers to their jobs. It didn't help that the housing he'd found for his community hardly lived up to its scenic English label. The advantage of Chalet Apartments was that no one objected to a dozen people living in a few rooms, but that hardly made up for the drug dealers and gangs that roamed the complex.

Exhaustion and worry for his people had become an integral part of Ye Win's daily life. How easy it would be to simply lay down his burden. Find a church where he could simply relax on

Sunday mornings. Concern himself with earning a good living for his own family. But leadership of the growing Karen community here in Smyrna was not just a responsibility Ye Win had taken on voluntarily. It was a deeply ingrained part of his heritage. A heritage he'd tried, but failed, to escape.

Born just two years before his younger brother Ga Nel Me, Ye Win's own father, John Kunoo, had followed a very different path than the well-known Karen National Liberation Army commander. The Karen people did not all, nor even the majority, live in KNLA-controlled territory. Many had taken refuge across the border in Thailand. But many others were scattered throughout Burmese towns and cities, especially in the south, and lived more or less assimilated into general Burmese society.

Like Ga Nel Me, John Kunoo had attended an Anglican high school, then university, where he received a teaching degree. He was teaching at a Christian high school in Papun when the government nationalized all schools. John was reluctant to continue teaching under the Burmese military regime, but the state's assistant governor, an ethnic Karen, begged him to continue.

"I know you don't want to work under the Burmese," he pleaded, "but would you be willing to work under me?"

John agreed. In time, he accepted a judgeship with the civil justice department as well. By now he was married, his wife, Daisy, also a schoolteacher. In time, John became a lay pastor and itinerant evangelist. Their different life paths kept John and Ga Nel Me apart for most of the next twenty years. In fact, the entire family was split into those who refused to join the armed conflict and those fighting with rebel forces in the jungle.

It was into this divided family, into this generations-long conflict of politics and faith that Ye Win was born in 1979. Perhaps if somehow he could help the Anglo vicar with whom he'd just met understand his story, the story of his people, they could find common ground. After all, the people of All Saints were Christ-followers too. That much Ye Win now knew at least. More so, they came from the same church heritage. They prayed from the same

Book of Common Prayer, followed the same liturgy, and sang the same hymns, even if in another language.

As though it wasn't enough to teach these Anglos about the Karen, the reverse was just as urgent. If Ye Win was to trust this Anglo church with the well-being of his family, his community, perhaps it would be wise as well to learn just who Father Michael Spurlock was and what had brought him to this crossroads of both their lives.

❄ ❄ ❄

While Michael Spurlock had been searching his entire life, he'd never realized it until he found the object of his search. Or, rather, was found.

Born in Knoxville, Tennessee, to teenage parents in 1968, Michael spent his early years bouncing from the custody of one parent or grandparent to another as his parents went through a difficult divorce. His paternal and maternal grandparents, with whom he occasionally lived, provided some semblance of stability that became an emotional safety net throughout his life. When Michael was six, his father remarried. While Michael cried when he learned he'd now be leaving his grandparents to live full-time with his father and stepmother, the stability and love they provided helped to heal some of the pain of divorce and uncertainty.

A more stable family life, however, was offset by the demands of his father's ever-more-successful career. While enjoying an increasingly prosperous lifestyle, the family suffered a series of ever-more-frequent transfers and relocations. By high school, Michael had lived all across the southeastern United States, along with stints in Chicago and Buffalo. Three years in Memphis was the longest Michael had been in any one school district, and in high school he actually attended a different school for each year.

Michael's sense of religious identity and faith was just as uprooted. He could not remember ever denying the existence of a supreme deity. His parents had grown up in Christian homes, his father in the Church of Christ, his mother and stepmother in the

Methodist Church. But by the time Michael was born, neither parent was attending church, and his only memories of church attendance in those early years were when he lived with his paternal grandparents.

When his father remarried, that changed. With each relocation, the family would seek out a church to attend, more often than not a Presbyterian church. It was in this church that Michael undertook catechism classes and his first communion. But with each successive move, it took longer to choose a new church, until some moves came and went with no church attendance at all (which was fine with Michael). In his younger years, he'd endured each new move resignedly, but with indifference. But as he reached his teens, he found it hard enough trying to fit in to a new town and school without being faced with a new church youth group. A newcomer like Michael was always welcomed to participate in youth activities, but that didn't necessarily translate to friendship when he ran into those same kids in school.

The hurt of this went deep, and with each new move, Michael found it more difficult to make new friends, whether at church, school, or within the neighborhood. He never discussed religion with his parents, as there seemed to be no point. But the constant shifting from poor Christian education to none at all left Michael with a distorted faith and a deficient knowledge of God.

Paramount was the concept that if God controlled everything, humanity was left without free will, whether to choose good or evil, which made religion a rigged system under which Michael could be condemned to hell for the slightest transgression—no matter how hard he tried to be good. If he so much as let a curse word slip into his thoughts, Michael felt overwhelmed with shame and fear, begging God to forgive him and not send him to hell.

Two incidents during his young religious development impacted him deeply. The first was a book his father had left in the back seat of their car: *The Late Great Planet Earth* by Hal Lindsey. On a road trip to Nashville, Michael read some of the book, but it was the back cover he never forgot. The back copy discouraged the reader from making any plans past the decade of the 1980s because, from what Michael understood, God was going to destroy the world by then. Doing the math, Michael realized his life would be over before it had hardly begun. It was a terrifying thought, not helped when his best friend's mom took them to watch the end-times movie *A Thief in the Night*. Intended to scare audiences into repentance before time ran out, it left Michael worried and terrified.

Coupled with a negative experience at his current youth group, these incidents strongly colored Michael's view of both God and the church. If he still believed in God, he neither liked nor trusted this Supreme Being who controlled the world and every aspect of his own life. Even worse, Michael's concept of God held nothing of a loving heavenly Father, only the punitive retribution of a harsh judge. And living in unrelenting fear of this God was exhausting.

What brought matters to a head was never clear to Michael. But walking down a high school corridor one day, he simply directed a mental outburst heavenward: *I'm not doing this anymore. I may believe in you, God, but I don't like you, and I'm not giving you power over my life anymore. From now on, I'm on my own!*

Another move shortly after this provided Michael the perfect escape. The family never did find a new church in their new location and rarely attended any other over the rest of Michael's high school years. By the time Michael left for college in 1986 to attend the University of Tennessee in Knoxville, he had no intentions of pursuing church attendance or any religious experience ever again.

6

A small boy growing up on the far side of the planet, Ye Win could not have agreed more. By the time he'd joined John and Daisy Kunoo's family, there were four older siblings, ages fifteen, thirteen, ten, and six. A much younger sister, Khin Kyi, was born in 1987.

Until the mid-1980s, the Kunoo family lived in Papun. Deep into Karen territory, Papun served for many years after World War II as headquarters of the Karen National Union (KNU) and its armed force (Karen National Liberation Army) KNLA. But by Ye Win's childhood, the Burmese military had taken control, the Karen rebel forces pushed back across the river and into the jungle, living a pedestrian life one step ahead of Burmese patrols and long-range mortars. This included plenty of Ye Win's own relatives. Ye Win remembers going to school in the morning, then sneaking across the river to spend an afternoon with Karen family members in the rebel forces.

In 1985, John Kunoo moved his family to Kamamaung City, still in Karen territory, but a safer distance from the front lines. But the 1980s became the decade that brought Myanmar's struggle for democracy to global attention. To the Burmese, the number eight is considered good fortune, so August 8, 1988 (8/8/88) was chosen for a nationwide pro-democracy general strike. Protestors included university students, doctors, lawyers, teachers, nursing unions, Muslims, Christians, Buddhist monks, Burman, Karen, and

Kachin, young and old. The protest turned deadly when military police were ordered to fire on the demonstrators, leaving uncounted fatalities across the country.

The uprising coincided with a visit from exile of pro-democracy activist Aung San Suu Kyi. Though she called for nonviolence in the struggle for democracy, the military placed her under house arrest for much of the following twenty years. They also unleashed a renewed campaign of shelling and burning villages, along with the usual atrocities of murder, torture, and rape. All of this affected the Karen conflict and Ye Win's own life story because it brought many Burmese, especially university students, into what had been primarily an ethnic minority revolution.

By now, Ye Win's father had become a pastor at a Baptist church in Kamamaung City. Shortly after, he gave up his judicial position to become a traveling evangelist. Ye Win's mother supported the family on her meager teacher's salary. An older brother and sister served as group leaders for Christian youth in the city until their activities drew attention from the military, forcing them to flee into the jungle. Ye Win's two other older siblings were already with the KNLA, along with countless cousins, uncles, and other relatives. One of Ye Win's sisters taught school to conflict orphans and refugee children. Another became a field nurse. Women as well as men fought on the front lines.

By the time Ye Win reached his teens, his four older brothers and sisters were all in the jungle. More than once, soldiers came to the Kunoo home in Kamamaung, insisting that John and Daisy were collaborating with rebels and demanding information on family members. They would leave only after shaking down Ye Win's mother for a bribe from her already scant teacher's salary, warning that they could come back at any time to kill the entire family.

Ye Win was now the only Kunoo child still at home except for his baby sister, Khin Kyi. His parents were determined that he would stay out of the conflict at least long enough to receive a good education, maybe even follow his father into the ministry. But by eighth grade, Ye Win was far less interested in his studies than the tales he heard from other family members of courageous battles against a cruel enemy, not to mention freedom and adventure in the jungle, while Ye Win lived restricted to school, church, and home. Other boys his age were already KLNA soldiers. Admittedly, they were war orphans taken in by the Karen army because they had nowhere else to go. Only the State Law and Order Restoration Council (SLORC) forced children to become soldiers.

Ye Win was also tired of poverty and hunger. While military surveillance was making it more difficult for his father to travel to outlying villages, many Karen were coming to Christ through John Kunoo's ministry, sometimes fifteen to twenty each week. Several new churches had resulted. But that didn't put food on the table, and what remained of his mother's teaching salary after keeping the soldiers at bay barely fed their family of four.

Strong and stocky for his age, Ye Win had become an amateur boxer and took every opportunity to learn martial arts. He had also grown increasingly rebellious against his parents' expectations for his future. Fighting for democracy sounded far more exciting than finishing high school and going on to study theology.

I will choose what I want to do in life, he vowed angrily.

❋ ❋ ❋

That had been Michael Spurlock's own axiom for years. Michael would later describe the years it took him to finish an undergraduate degree at the University of Tennessee as the most willful years of his life. For a major, he wavered between creative writing and philosophy. When he couldn't find in his scant two decades of life experience a satisfactory story to fill the pages of the next "great American novel," he shifted to fine arts with an emphasis on painting. But his attempts to tell a story through painting proved as devoid of meaning and purpose as that earlier novel.

Years later, Michael would recognize he'd simply not found a story worthy of devoting his time and energy to writing, painting, telling, or living. Now in his early twenties, he hadn't attended church in years. But somehow living life by his own wits and according to his own will hadn't proved as liberating as he'd expected.

One day while listening to National Public Radio, Michael listened with unusual interest to a news story about an appearance of the Virgin Mary somewhere in the Midwest that was attracting pilgrims from all over the United States, if not the world. As he listened to declarations of devotion and faith from various pilgrims, Michael told himself unexpectedly, *I wish I had that kind of faith.*

The thought led to a new impulse: *I want to go back to church.* Why, Michael had no idea. None of his friends attended church. But the impulse became a persistent longing, then a determination.

Michael's one resolve was that he would not allow sentiment to drive him back to the religion of his childhood. Conducting his search as an academic query, Michael began researching the origins of Christianity and the church. His investigation led him to Roman Catholicism.

Searching out the nearest parish church, Michael began attending Sunday mass. The officiating priest spoke of God's love, a new concept for Michael. He also spoke of Jesus in a way that was completely new to Michael. Not a defenseless baby in a manger. Not a capricious tyrant or manipulator of defenseless creatures. Nor the sentimental figure Michael remembered from poorly rendered Sunday school lessons. This Jesus knew exactly what flawed, sinful humanity was all about but had chosen to give his life for them anyway.

The fact that Jesus didn't have to die, but did so of his own free will, hit Michael with a weight he'd never before grasped. For so long, Michael had seen God as exercising absolute control, humanity simply an automaton beholden to his capricious will. But Jesus had given his life freely. He had truly lived, truly suffered, truly died, and truly come back from the dead.

And he now offered Michael the free choice to accept or reject the forgiveness and redemption for which Michael had so yearned and believed he could never attain. This was a Jesus Michael could believe in. This was what he'd been searching for. This was *who* he'd been searching for.

Week after week, Michael went back to church. He also began to pray as he had never prayed before in his life. He studied church history, learned the criteria for becoming a Roman Catholic, and attended mass. He even mulled over the possibility of becoming a Catholic priest. That lasted only as long as it took Michael to remind himself that he wanted a wife and family someday.

It was during this time of spiritual exploration that Michael finally earned his college degree. He was tired of studying, tired of struggling financially, and sick of making paintings that felt completely devoid of meaning. With the optimism of youth, he decided to move to New York City and enter the field of publishing. With any luck, he might become the next Max Perkins, famed as the editor who'd discovered Ernest Hemingway, F. Scott Fitzgerald, and Thomas Wolfe. In his spare time, he might still churn out that great American novel.

In 1993, now twenty-five years old, Michael bought a one-way ticket from Nashville to New York City. He found work through a temp agency and within a year had been hired as editorial assistant in HarperCollins' college textbook division, a position that lasted through two mergers and a promotion to assistant editor. He was still praying and had found a neighborhood church to attend, if less regularly.

But he was not happy. He hated the city's frenetic pace of life and was strongly considering taking any job that would get him back out of the city. It was a chance encounter, if such a thing exists, that changed Michael's life forever. An encounter that would place him on a path leading through valleys and mountains and deserts—and ultimately to a small country church named All Saints in his birth state of Tennessee.

7

Twelve time zones away, Ye Win had made up his mind about his own life path. He knew good and well what his parents' reaction would be, so he didn't bother asking permission before joining several friends to sneak out of town and through the jungle to the rebel front. He was now thirteen years old, and he would not see his parents again for more than two years.

Uncle Ga Nel Me was not part of the front Ye Win joined, but another uncle was a KLNA commander with six thousand troops under him. Over the following years, Ye Win learned to use weapons from AK-47s and M16 assault rifles to rocket-propelled grenade (RPG) launchers and M60 machine guns. He learned to plant land mines on trails and in fields frequented by the Burmese military. He also learned to kill without hesitation. To ignore the smell of blood and death. To close his ears to the thunder of gunfire. To close his mind to the screams of the wounded.

Despite their youth, Ye Win and his friends were sent to the front lines to face Burmese troops, sometimes in small units of a dozen or less, sometimes as part of a larger brigade column. When the shooting started, Ye Win had to battle fear, but once his own weapon came up, adrenaline banished any thought but combat. Rebel troops fought mostly under cover of the jungle canopy and underbrush, which often meant hunkering down for hours without ever seeing the enemy. Then sunlight would catch on a metallic rifle barrel or reflect from safety goggles, and Ye Win would empty his weapon in that direction.

The fighting was not continuous. Dry season permitted both Burmese and rebel troops to move freely. In rainy season, torrential downpours, flooding, and landslides made travel unpleasant and dangerous. These were the months for settling in among sympathetic Karen villages, planting crops, holding school, and resting up for the next fighting season.

By this time Ye Win had made his first border crossing into Thailand. The war had not gone well for the KNLA in recent years, and their front had been pushed back by the Burmese military closer and closer to the Salween River that formed the border between the two countries. Hundreds of thousands of Karen, burned out of villages and farms, had taken shelter across the border, where the United Nations High Commissioner for Refugees (UNHCR) supported a number of refugee camps, housing not only Karen, but Kachin, Shin, Cambodian, Laotian, and other refugee populations. Rebel troops flowed back and forth across the border, ignored for the most part by Thai government forces.

It was in Thailand that Ye Win's parents finally caught up with him. They had managed to track down his whereabouts through various family members in KNLA command. They sent a messenger across the border to the jungle camp where Ye Win was currently stationed, pleading for his return.

Now fifteen, Ye Win was more than ready to accede. He'd grown tired of the constant marching, fighting, heat, and rain. Nor had the food turned out to be more plentiful than back at home, the troops often fighting all day on no more than a fist-sized ball of cold rice dabbed with fish paste and wrapped in a banana leaf. Besides, even his superior officers were counseling him as to the value of finishing his education.

In 1994, Ye Win returned home. Within two years, he had finished his secondary education (Myanmar follows the British system of ten standard grades, followed by matriculation exams for university). By now, he considered himself as much a pan-Burmese democracy activist as a Karen resistance fighter. In December 1996, he heard that pro-democracy leader Aung San Suu Kyi had been freed from house arrest. With a group of friends, Ye Win headed to Rangoon to hear Aung San Suu Kyi speak and offer support to the democracy movement.

When Ye Win arrived, fresh student protests were filling the streets of Rangoon. As in 1988, the military response was swift. Aung San Suu Kyi was again confined to her compound. Army tanks and armored personnel carriers filled with soldiers surrounded the crowds of students. This time they turned water cannons and batons, rather than bullets, on the students. But hundreds were rounded up and arrested.

Ye Win found himself on the run. He could not get back to his parents in Kamamaung, so he headed straight across country to Karen territory, where he knew he could take refuge with KNLA family members. But rather than shelter, Ye Win found himself in a war zone as the Burmese army again declared a scorched-earth policy against the Karen as well as any other pro-democracy elements.

Ye Win was handed a weapon and assigned an army unit. At age seventeen, he was once again a soldier. While he'd been able to get word to his parents that he'd escaped Rangoon, threats against their own lives had driven them from Kamamaung. Ye Win had no idea where they'd gone, nor did they know his whereabouts. His brothers and sisters were scattered to the winds as well.

Ye Win could not have guessed that this time he would not see his parents or siblings again for almost a decade. Nor that their reunion would be on the far side of the planet.

❄ ❄ ❄

For Michael Spurlock, a sharp turn in his life journey began with a tap on the shoulder. He'd met up with a friend in New York City's Central Park. They were engaged in an admittedly trivial discussion on the finer differences between bourbon and sour mash whiskey as produced in the Kentucky and Tennessee hills of Michael's youth when he felt the tap. Then the voice of an angel—or a trained musician—broke in on their conversation. "Excuse me? My friend would like to know more of what you are talking about."

Turning, Michael saw a young woman whose beauty matched her voice. She was petite, brunette, with luxurious curls framing a heart-shaped face. If Michael had ever doubted the existence of love at first sight, he did so no longer. He felt as though he'd been struck by a lightning bolt.

The young woman was now introducing her friend, who really did have a genuine interest in the differences between bourbon and sour mash. Michael was suddenly and completely disinterested in the topic. What was this young woman's name?

"Aimee," she informed him. "Aimee Marcoux."

Michael was just as suddenly and completely no longer interested in escaping the Big Apple.

8

Born in Miami Beach, Florida, in 1966, Aimee Marcoux knew her calling in life before she was old enough to read. God had created her to make music and to serve him. What could be more clear?

Her musical talent had been pointed out from the time her pure, soaring voice had drawn notice from family, church, and school. By age five, she performed her first singing role as a child extra in the musical *Hello, Dolly!* At age six, Aimee's performance as Captain von Trapp's youngest daughter, Gretl, in *The Sound of Music* led to offers of roles in commercials, television, and other shows. Not wanting such a life for their daughter's childhood, her parents turned them all down, focusing instead on ensuring that she received a top-notch classical music education.

Devout Christians, Aimee's parents were prominently involved in a local Episcopal church. Aimee sang in the church choir and in the choir of a nearby Presbyterian church as well. The Presbyterian church also sponsored a touring high school choir, founded on the prestigious Royal School of Church Music program. Its reputation drew concert invites all across North America as well as Europe. By college, Aimee had sung her way across Switzerland, Germany, Austria, England, and France.

Choir directors Bill and Katie Stevenson were not just instructors but mentors to their teenage protégés. Beyond good singing, the life lessons they taught would stand Aimee in good stead for the rest of her life. How to be punctual, prepared, and respectful. How to be quiet and listen. Above all, to know who it was she was singing to and for. Not a rapt audience, but God himself.

But once Aimee left home for the University of Miami, both church attendance and faith moved to a back burner. She spent a summer at the Chautauqua Institution, a fine arts program in upstate New York, singing in their opera company. By summer's end, Aimee was hooked. This world held so much more than a tame return to studies in Miami. She auditioned at the Boston Conservatory of Music, where she received a full scholarship. After graduating in 1987, she went on to complete a master's degree in classical opera. She sang operas, festivals, and oratorios with orchestras and opera companies across the United States and even in Germany.

But her personal life was not proving so successful. Her parents had expressed concern at the type of men she was dating. Her latest boyfriend didn't share her Christian faith, and for the first time Aimee was wondering if it would really be so wrong to leave her own church, even convert to another religion, in order to build a life with the man she loved.

Her mother vociferously disagreed. "Whatever you choose, how can you turn your back on Jesus Christ? You can't do that!"

I'm losing myself, Aimee recognized reluctantly. *What made me think I could just switch myself out for another person? It isn't right!*

Then disaster struck. Or, as Aimee recognized many years later, God intervened. One evening in 1994, Aimee had sung the National Anthem for a Miami Marlins game. As she drove home from the baseball stadium, a drunk driver ran a red light, hitting Aimee head-on. The impact sent Aimee's vehicle into a 360-degree spin and fractured her jaw in two places. Three reconstructive surgeries followed. With her jaw wired shut, eating was difficult, and Aimee became alarmingly thin. Both her career and her romantic relationship appeared to be over. Her parents were at least happy about the latter.

Aimee herself sunk into deep depression. Music had been her world. What was she to do with the rest of her life? Her answer came through a phone call from New York City. The caller was a friend who'd been an assistant conductor at the Metropolitan Opera. He was heading to Houston to work with their Grand Opera for a season or two and didn't want to lose his rent-controlled apartment on the Upper West Side. Would Aimee like to take over the lease while he was gone?

To Aimee, this was no serendipitous invite, but a sign from God himself. God had opened a door and was giving her an opportunity to start over. Just what she'd do in New York City, she had no idea. She had $1,500 in savings. Buying a plane ticket, she arrived in New York, paid her first month's rent, and bought a few groceries. Now to find a job.

That very evening, a number of friends from her music career threw Aimee a "Welcome to NYC" party. Among the guests was Russell Granger, a former television director and co-founder of the brand-new Entertainment Drive, an online company focused on entertainment news as well as PR marketing for the entertainment industry and television networks. All this Aimee discovered before Russell asked about her own plans.

"I need a job," Aimee answered simply.

"Oddly enough, I need an assistant," Russell responded.

By the end of the party, Aimee had a new friend, a boss, and a job. Along with her duties as Russell's assistant, she became Entertainment Drive's first online reporter. Though she had no prior experience, the same golden voice and training that made her a success as a singer made her a natural on camera.

Over the next years, Aimee interviewed such celebrities as Anthony Hopkins, Denzel Washington, Secretary-General of the UN Kofi Annan, and President Bill Clinton. She also covered the Emmys and Oscars. In early 1997, she began freelancing as well for Showtime and eventually Reuters, BBC, NBC, and CBS, among others. Her jaw had finally healed, and she began singing again, though she was enjoying her current job too much to go back to the constant travel and repetitive work of a full-time opera career.

On June 29, 1997, Aimee was strolling through Central Park with Russell Granger, no longer her boss, but still a good friend. She'd recently gone through another romantic breakup and was expressing her disgust with the New York City dating scene. As they walked, Aimee vocalized her wish list. "I want a man with a great sense of humor. Someone from the South with real manners. Someone intelligent, who will let *me* be intelligent."

One attribute Aimee did not mention was good looks. After the last few years in Hollywood's tinsel reality, that was no longer a priority. But she added, "And I want a Christian, someone who will share my faith."

The latter had taken on more importance since Aimee had recently met a young, newly ordained Episcopal priest on a train ride. He'd just received his first assignment as an assistant at Grace Church, a parish in lower Manhattan. Aimee had accepted his invitation to visit and was now attending church regularly for the first time in many years.

But Aimee's companion was not paying attention to her musings. "Be quiet, Aimee. I'm trying to hear what that man has to say."

"What man?"

Russell gestured to a man, tallish, slimly fit, in a baseball cap and teal-colored shirt, chatting with another man just a few yards ahead. Shyness never being one of Aimee's debilities, she stepped forward immediately and tapped on the teal-colored shoulder. "Excuse me, sir. My friend here wants to know what you're talking about."

Swinging around, the man went on without skipping a beat, "Well, the difference between bourbon and sour mash . . ."

Aimee couldn't care less. What she noticed were the most beautiful eyes she'd ever seen in her life, the lilting southern accent, that this man was both articulate and kind-natured. *He's my wish list!*

"Michael Spurlock," the stranger said, introducing himself. He quickly fell into conversation with Aimee. Russell and Michael's own companion finally excused themselves.

For the next two hours, it felt as though time had stopped. Michael spoke of his publishing career, dreams of writing, indifference to painting. Aimee found herself opening up about the tragedy that had interrupted her singing career. They talked about where they were from, where they'd gone to college. Most important to Aimee, Michael shared of his reconciliation with God, his growing faith in Jesus Christ.

The urgency of other appointments finally broke into their bubble. Michael was quick to ask for Aimee's phone number and give her a card with his own. Aimee was touched when Michael insisted on walking her to the subway and purchasing a token to drop into the toll slot. After three years in the city, she'd been chauffeured around in limousines, wined and dined at expensive restaurants. But none of those seemed as romantic as Michael's simple gesture of courtesy.

When Aimee agreed to a dinner date, they again talked for hours with the same ease as their first encounter. It occurred to Aimee she'd never met a man like this, who showed more interest in Aimee's thoughts, heart, and soul than the sultry flare of her orange frock and her carefully cultivated beauty. That he also possessed a delightful drawl and southern charm was just a bonus.

Here is a man who would love me, Aimee Marcoux, not the celebrity persona who has to look and be perfect on and off camera. Who might actually respect me for my intelligence and personality, not just see me as eye candy to make him look good!

By the end of dinner, neither had any doubt this was a relationship worth pursuing. Less than six months after that chance encounter in Central Park, on December 18, 1997, Michael Spurlock and Aimee Marcoux Gaus were married in Grace Church by the young priest Aimee had met on the subway.

9

Michael and Aimee were both committed to finding a partner with whom they could share a life of faith, but they came from very different church traditions. Since Aimee couldn't receive Communion in the Roman Catholic Church, and there was no such restriction for Michael in the Episcopal Church, they decided to attend Grace Church together.

They also approached Aimee's friend about performing their marriage ceremony. The Rev. William J. Danaher, Bill to his friends, turned out to be a young man close in age to Michael himself. Like Aimee, his wife, Claire, was a gifted musician. But sparks immediately flew when Father Bill laid out the requirements for Aimee and Michael to be married at Grace Church. Along with premarital counseling, the couple was asked to attend a young adult prayer group Father Bill was starting. Michael's hackles immediately rose.

"I came down to meet with you to plan our wedding ceremony, not join a prayer meeting," Michael told the priest flatly. "This is my wedding. It will be done my way."

Father Bill met Michael's defiant glare with a level gaze. Quietly, but firmly, he responded, "You strike me as someone who has done it your way your whole life. I wonder, how's that been working out for you? I wonder what would happen if you tried it the Grace way. God's way. Maybe you ought to think about that."

Michael was fuming as he and Aimee left the church and boarded the subway back uptown. What kind of jerk was this priest to be telling Michael how he should get married? They were adult professionals, not kids out of high school! Aimee, in contrast, had little to say.

But then it began to dawn on Michael what he sounded like. *Me . . . me . . . me! My . . . my . . . my!* He shut up. After a silence, he turned to Aimee. "You know, I've insisted on my way my whole life. I guess I've really been saying no to God my whole life. I wonder what would happen if I said yes instead. Maybe it is time to try something different."

They returned to Aimee's apartment, and Michael went straight for the telephone. Calling Father Bill back, Michael said, "I have thought about what you said in our meeting. You were right. I have been doing things my own way for a long time now, and the results have not been very good. I'm ready and willing to try it God's way. What do we need to do?"

First, they needed to attend the prayer group Bill mentioned. So they went, Michael still reluctant, Aimee excited. A circle of chairs was filled with young men and women in their twenties. After a Bible study on the parables of Jesus came a time of intercessory prayer. People began sharing needs and praises, praying out loud together. Michael had never experienced anything like this. A flood of emotion swept over him. He hadn't wanted to come here. Now he didn't want to leave.

The prayer group marked a turning point in Michael's life. Though he'd researched the Catholic Church, and taken confirmation classes, he'd never actually studied the Bible. Now he purchased one and began reading it through, starting with the Gospel of John.

"I can't believe I never knew any of this!" he kept exclaiming to Aimee as he read.

"When I became a Catholic, I was converted to the church," Michael reminisces today. "It was when Aimee and I began attending Grace Church that I found the Bible, and was truly converted to Jesus."

By the time Michael and Aimee were married, they counted Father Bill and Claire among their closest friends. More so, Michael found in Bill Danaher a role model. Here was someone his own age who'd had a successful career in politics in Connecticut before giving it up to go to seminary. Michael was reminded of his own earlier ambitions of entering the priesthood. When he saw Father Bill officiating the Eucharist at the altar, he could see himself there. Maybe entering the ministry wasn't such a pipe dream after all.

❀ ❀ ❀

For Ye Win, life had taken a far different and less pleasant turn. By the late 1990s, the KNLA resistance had proved unable to maintain territorial hold against the Burmese army. Karen now poured over the Thai border into refugee camps. Remaining units like Ye Win's fought a desperate rear-guard battle as the Burmese extended their scorched-earth campaign deeper and deeper into Karen territory.

At the time nineteen-year-old Ye Win lay shivering from malaria and fevered with infection in a refugee camp clinic, almost two hundred thousand Karen were living in nine refugee camps along the Thai-Burmese border, along with hundreds of thousands of other ethnicities, including pro-democracy Burmese elements. An estimated two million more had been internally displaced in Myanmar itself, due to the destruction of their homes and villages.

At first Thailand, already dealing with communist neighbors in Cambodia, Laos, and China, welcomed the refugees and rebel resistance as a buffer between their own right-wing regime and the Chinese-socialist leaning military junta in Rangoon. But as refugees continued to pour in, Thailand's huge refugee population became more a liability than an asset. While the UNHCR continued funneling aid to the camps, the Thai government branded the refugees as "people without a state," denying identification papers that would allow them to make a new life outside the camps, essentially consigning them to an indefinite "camp arrest."

None of this concerned Ye Win, since, like other rebels, he simply ignored border demarcations and government demands on either side of the Thai-Burmese border. The day after he'd cried out for God's intervention, he awoke in the refugee camp clinic still weak, but alive and without a fever. Within a few weeks, he'd regained his strength. Hearing of Ye Win's recovery, a KNLA commander sent a secret message ordering Ye Win to report back to duty. Now there appeared a significant crossroads. Would God answer his desperate plea, or would he have to return to the fighting and killing?

In all his years separated from family and church, Ye Win had not lost his belief in God. But he had certainly lost faith that God cared enough about him personally to intervene on his behalf as God had done in the days of Abraham, Moses, King David, and other Old Testament heroes. So it was with stunned amazement that Ye Win received his new assignment. He wasn't being ordered back to the front, but to the Thai capital, Bangkok.

"We are never going to win our freedom through fighting," the KNLA commander told Ye Win. "It is time to seek a political solution. You have a good education. In school, you learned Thai and Burmese as well as Karen. You are smart enough to learn English. We need you to be our representative to speak to the UNHCR and Western embassies on our behalf."

Thank you, Lord God, Ye Win prayed. God had answered his prayers and intervened to set his life on a new path. Now Ye Win renewed his vow to serve God for the rest of his life.

In all, six young Karen soldiers were chosen for the trip. One was already fluent in English and helped tutor the others. Reaching Bangkok, the group sought out the Burmese student center, already headquarters for Myanmar's pro-democracy activists. For the next five years, Ye Win would remain in Bangkok as liaison and spokesman for the Karen.

10

ichael Spurlock once again dreamed of becoming a priest like Father Bill, but he was all too well aware that he now had a family to support. Not long after Michael and Aimee were married, the publishing company Michael worked for went through its third merger in as many years. Michael's own job survived all the reshuffling, but the instability made him nervous.

Now Aimee was pregnant. In the summer of 1999, the Spurlocks welcomed the birth of their son, Atticus. Neither Michael nor Aimee wanted to raise a family in the big city, so they decided to move back to Tennessee. Nashville had a thriving publishing industry, especially in the Christian market, so Michael felt confident he could find similar work there.

Sure enough, Michael was hired as marketing director for R. H. Boyd Publishing Company, a publisher of Sunday school curriculum and other material for a large African-American Baptist denomination. Aimee had also returned to work part-time as a freelance journalist, occasionally flying back to New York to cover assigned stories on fashion shows and other events. She was preparing for a fashion segment on *Good Morning America* the morning of September 11, 2001. Receiving a call from her producer to cover a plane crash at the World Trade Center, Aimee grabbed her cameraman, and together they headed downtown. She had just enough time to call her family back in Tennessee to let them know where she was going.

Aimee would never forget the terror of running from the collapsing Trade Center, the police screaming at her to run for her life, her fear that she would never see her husband and son again. Michael would never forget watching the towers collapse on television, knowing that his wife was reporting from the site. It was only later that night that Aimee was able to get in touch with him to let him know that she was alive. Over the following days, she remained on-site. Her coverage of the terror attack and its aftermath won her a Royal Television Society award.

With a stable job and beautiful wife and son, Michael's life would seem complete. But the idea of attending seminary was becoming a nagging thought. Michael reminded himself of all the reasons such an idea was impractical, if not crazy. He'd just found a new position. He had a family to support. Another major move wouldn't be fair to Aimee. He was too old to go back to school.

There was another reason such a move was out of the question. Aimee was dealing with severe health issues of her own. While still in New York, she'd been training to run a marathon when she noticed that her left foot kept going numb, then her left hand as well. She'd dismissed it as too-tight running shoes, a glove that cut off circulation. After Atticus's birth, she'd never recovered her energy, but wasn't that normal with a new baby? Then one day while Aimee was grocery shopping, a store clerk ran into her with a pallet piled high with merchandise. The impact was hard enough to send Aimee to the hospital. That was when a neurologist discovered her symptoms were actually the beginning stage of multiple sclerosis.

It was an unforgettable Friday afternoon when Aimee learned of her diagnosis. The specialist was not noted for his bedside manner. Brusquely, he informed Aimee, "Look, you're a reporter. You're used to processing bad news. So I'm just going to come out and say it. In five years, you'll be using a walker. In ten years, you'll be in a wheelchair. I'm not going to be in the office again till Monday."

You're smart. Just go on the Internet and check out the facts. If you still have any questions, call me on Monday."

This was devastating news. Atticus was still an infant. Was this doctor saying that when her son was five years old, he'd have a mother using a walker? *I don't think so!* Aimee vowed. And she kept that vow. Medication, a strict diet and exercise regimen, and, above all, the power of prayer were what Aimee credited for the full remission she eventually experienced. But who knew how long that remission might last?

Their friend Bill Danaher had left Grace Church and was now on faculty at a nearby seminary. A visit to the campus only increased Michael's yearning. He determined to ask Aimee what she thought about his quitting his job to attend seminary and become a priest. If her response was a flat-out no, he'd drop the idea.

But Aimee didn't say no. She'd never forgotten their first conversation when Michael had shared his early impulse to become a Catholic priest. She also saw in him the yearning and gifting to be a spiritual shepherd to others. The thought of losing a steady income and house, of her MS flaring up, should have aroused fear and worry. But she felt absolute peace.

"Who am I to argue with the Holy Spirit?" Aimee told Michael. "Let's do it."

※ ※ ※

Twelve time zones away in Bangkok, Ye Win was no longer a teenager, but a young man who'd become as expert at maneuvering through diplomatic and political minefields as he was at handling an AK-47 or RPG launcher. He'd spoken before the UN refugee committee, met with humanitarian non-governmental organizations (NGOs) to advocate the refugee plight. He'd traveled back across the Burmese border to lead other refugee groups to safety. He'd also attended school, studying English and political science.

Though he was no longer fighting, Ye Win was not staying out of trouble. Many Burmese pro-democracy activists—Burman, Karen, Kachin, Shin—were living in exile in Bangkok. Most militant were the university-age youth. Ye Win became the leader of one such group. To publicize the plight of the Burmese people, they held demonstrations and sit-ins outside Myanmar's embassy in Bangkok, avidly filmed by international news crews from CNN, Associated Press, Reuters, and others. Along with other agitators, Ye Win found himself on a Thai government blacklist.

This did not become a problem until 2002. Many of Ye Win's family members had left Myanmar for refugee camps inside Thailand. The overflowing camps and international attention had in turn led to a UN-sponsored refugee settlement program. Ye Win's uncle, Ga Nel Me, and some of Ye Win's siblings had already been resettled to Australia. Through other family members, Ye Win had located his parents and younger sister in Hpa-an City back in Myanmar. Many Karen refugees had spent almost two decades in the camps with no end in sight. The family consensus was that the time had come for the Kunoo family to forge a new life in a new country.

But when Ye Win applied for refugee status, he was told that the Thai government had listed him as a political rabble-rouser and was blocking his emigration. Over the next two years, various friends and family members left Thailand, but Ye Win's request for an exit visa was repeatedly denied. The Thai government warned Ye Win that his only path to a refugee visa was to renounce any further political activism. But it was not in Ye Win's nature to let despotic authorities intimidate him into silence.

I don't care! Ye Win told himself. *I'm single. It will make no difference to anyone if I don't emigrate. I'll just stay here and continue fighting for freedom.*

11

Becoming an Episcopal priest is not an overnight process. Once accepted as a candidate for ordained ministry, Michael began the long process of interviews and evaluation. It was 2003 when the letter of recommendation arrived, approving Michael to study for the priesthood.

The question now was which seminary to attend. Both Michael and Aimee were from the South, and leaving behind the bitter cold and snow had been a major perk of their move from New York. So of eleven seminaries, there was only one both Michael and Aimee immediately determined was not an option—Nashotah House Theological Seminary, located outside Milwaukee near Lake Michigan in frigid Wisconsin. When Michael made their request known to the bishop overseeing his ordination, he was shocked at the response. "No, we want you to go to Wisconsin."

In time, Michael understood the reasoning. Nashotah House was known for its unwavering commitment to the authority of Scripture and tradition. Such a strong foundation was what the bishop was seeking for new clergy who would be serving in their diocese. But it was an unexpected blow, especially since Michael knew what Aimee's reaction would be.

"Okay," he answered the bishop simply. Then he added, "What if we hate it?"

"Just go and visit," the bishop told him. "If you absolutely hate it, we can talk about another option. But I think you will thrive there, and this is my choice for you. At least check it out."

Michael called Aimee and asked her to meet him at a local restaurant. When he told her of the bishop's decision, she began to cry. From a nearby table, they overheard two older women whispering to each other, "I think they're getting a divorce!"

"Look, he just wants us to visit," Michael assured Aimee. "If we tell him we hate it, they'll send us somewhere else."

The trip was scheduled for February, the temperature bitterly cold, the snow deep, as the Spurlocks drove from Tennessee to Wisconsin. Beyond the weather issue was a mutual fear that this dream of seminary and ministry was simply more than they could handle. But from the moment Michael and Aimee stepped onto the grounds of Nashotah House, its beautiful setting, the communal life, its emphasis on daily prayer and worship all combined to win them over completely. Upon their return to Nashville, Michael wrote a note to the bishop: "Thank you for sending us to Nashotah. We've just concluded a wonderful visit. If you gave us permission now to attend elsewhere, we wouldn't take you up on the offer."

❄ ❄ ❄

During this same period, Ye Win was again in the Thai news for leading strikes and demonstrations. While he had never forgotten his vow to serve God, he had not actively pursued his faith or church attendance since arriving in Bangkok. After all, his sacrifices in agitating for democracy must certainly count as serving God and others. By 2004, Ye Win had finished the interview process for a refugee visa to the United States, but he hadn't pursued the visa as he still hoped to join his uncle and older siblings in Australia.

"Just take the visa to the United States," family members urged him.

Before he could do so, Ye Win was arrested, along with several dozen other protestors, and thrown into the Bangkok detention center, infamous for its hellish conditions with up to a hundred prisoners in a cell and minimal food and water. Many prisoners had no political affiliation but were simply refugees caught outside the camps without papers.

Thai authorities made clear that Ye Win's only alternative to prison was being deported back to Rangoon, where the Burmese military would likely execute him. Despairing, Ye Win began to pray. *I have no chance. There is no way now I can get into any other country. And if they send me back to Burma, my life is over. Please, God, if you will help me, I will make no more excuses. I will serve you. I will do your work.*

By now, Ye Win was dating a young Karen refugee. He asked her to bring him a Bible. When she did, he began reading. Conditions did not improve in his crowded cell, but he was no longer in despair.

Ye Win soon discovered that there were several other Christian families among the refugees in his cell. He began praying with them. Many of the refugees were illiterate or had no Bible of their own, so he began reading the Bible to them as well. As he read, much of what Ye Win had learned as a child from Sunday school and his father's preaching came back to him, and he began sharing this as well with the other prisoners. A Bible study developed right in the cell. Even Buddhist prisoners, with little else for entertainment, joined the group. A month passed, then two. Ye Win's situation remained just as hopeless, but his faith was growing. Whatever happened, God was with him.

Then, just as when he'd first cried out to God in that refugee camp clinic, something happened that could be nothing less than God's direct intervention. A visiting UN inspection team stopped by Ye Win's crowded cell. They were interviewing prisoners, specifically those whose political activism placed them at risk if sent back to their birth country. They wanted to talk to the leader of the arrested student activists.

When Ye Win was identified as the leader, they asked how many were in his group. By now, some of his colleagues who possessed passports or work permits had been released. Others in the cell were active rebel soldiers, who were not eligible for release. That left a group of about thirty men, women, and children for whom Ye Win had taken responsibility.

"These are all with me," Ye Win told the UN officials.

"Then you need to write a letter," they responded, "asking for political asylum instead of regular refugee status, since you face danger from the Burmese government if you are deported back there."

Ye Win prayed as he wrote the letter. The UN visit was already a miracle. Surely his release was now at hand. But when the UN team returned, it was with the news that the others were free to leave Thailand to any country participating in the refugee resettlement. But Ye Win had already defied several warnings to stop political demonstrations. The Thai authorities were refusing to let him leave. The UN officials promised to keep pushing for Ye Win's release.

For the next ten days, Ye Win prayed. Then a UN representative came to the prison. He said to Ye Win bluntly, "I believe you are not a bad person, whatever your record. We can get you out of here, but only if you promise to be involved in no further political demonstrations or statements to the media. Just keep quiet and leave the country."

Ye Win had absolutely no doubt it was God who had opened the prison door for him. God was making clear his path for Ye Win's life and it did not include remaining in Thailand.

"I will be quiet," he agreed. And he kept his word. As soon as he was released, Ye Win headed straight for the American Embassy.

"Your name is clear," he was told. "You've already finished your interviews and passed a physical exam. You'll have to undergo a three-day orientation. Then you will be put on a flight to the United States."

Ye Win made one last attempt with the UN official. "What if I apply to Australia now that my name is off the blacklist?"

The UN official didn't beat around the bush. "Don't even think of starting this all over again! If you apply again to Australia, you'll lose the visa to the United States, and there is no guarantee you'll be cleared to go to Australia. Just take the United States visa and get out of here."

Ye Win took it as an answer from God. He'd promised God he'd do what God wanted. It was now clear that God wanted him to go to the United States. His visa allowed for a spouse, so before boarding the plane, he married his girlfriend in a simple Karen ceremony. Three days later, their plane touched down in North Carolina.

Ye Win was free, but along with war, oppression, and imprisonment, he'd also left behind his country, people, family, and all that was familiar. Was there a place in this vast new country called the United States for a Karen refugee like him to build a new life and home?

12

For the next three years, Nashotah House became home to the Spurlock family. The student body was small, less than a hundred all told, and all students lived in community on campus. Each day started with prayer together in the chapel, breakfast together, classes, noon worship, and lunch together, then chores. All was punctuated three times each day by the tolling of Nashotah's one-ton bell, auspiciously named Michael.

The second year, Atticus started kindergarten. As Aimee had vowed, she walked him to the bus stop. In fact, despite her condition, she worked two jobs to help support the family during Michael's seminary years. In her scant free time, she founded Nashotah House's first children's choir, based on the Royal School of Church Music.

Even with Aimee working, finances were tight. But both Michael and Aimee were learning to trust that if God had brought them to this place, he would also care for their needs. During the second year, their single vehicle broke down. The repair bill was $250, but they only had $40 in the bank. Praying over the situation, Michael walked down to the mailbox. There he found a check for $250.

Another year, three unexpected financial expenses occurred at once. They needed a minimum of $400 to cover expenses. Picking up their mail, Michael discovered another check for $500. Then their biggest financial crisis came when their old vehicle blew its transmission. The bill was a whopping $1,500. By now Michael wasn't wasting time on worry.

"I'm going to the mailbox," he told Aimee. Sure enough, God had provided. A Nashville church regularly gave a gift to a seminary student. Since their current rector had studied at Nashotah, this year the gift was earmarked there. The choice of student: Michael Spurlock. The gift: exactly $1,500.

Their vehicle, which Michael's parents had given him years earlier, was an old Ford Explorer with extremely high mileage. But there were no funds for an upgrade. Michael began praying over the car, "Lord, please let the car at least get us through seminary."

When Michael finally graduated and the Spurlocks headed back to Tennessee, the Explorer putted along all the way through Nashville. They'd just pulled off the exit to their new home in Murfreesboro, Tennessee, a few miles south of Nashville, when something came loose and the vehicle began bucking and kicking. Michael was able to coax it into their driveway before it finally died. God had answered his prayer. They would now have to buy a vehicle, but they also could afford it for the first time in three years.

Those lessons in trusting God would be much needed in the future.

One other significant incident occurred during Michael's first year of seminary. The primary speaker at an academic convocation he attended was Baroness Caroline Cox from the UK, a devoutly Christian human rights activist who would become well-known for her relief efforts among the Karen and other refugee groups from Myanmar. At the conference, she mentioned neither the Karen nor Myanmar, but she shared stories of the persecuted church in Sudan, Indonesia, and other totalitarian countries.

The story that most impacted Michael was that of young Christian students in Indonesia whose Sunday school teacher had taken them on a camping trip. The group was ambushed by jihadists, who eviscerated the leader in front of his students. They then seized one student, demanding that he deny Christ as his Savior. When the boy refused, the jihadists chopped off one arm. Their leader told the boy, "Look, we don't want to hurt you. If you'll just renounce Christianity, we'll spare all of you."

"I belong to Christ," the boy responded. "There is nothing else to tell you."

The jihadists proceeded to chop off the boy's other arm. When he still refused to renounce his faith, they eviscerated him too. Upon being interrupted by a group of cattle herders, the jihadists climbed into their truck and drove off, leaving the rest of the class alive to report the atrocities.

The story was simply told, but its combination of horror, bravery, conviction, faith, and the life-and-death nature of these young boys' decision to follow Christ left Michael weeping uncontrollably. A Nashotah faculty member followed up with a somber statement: "Just take a look around you and consider which of you might be called to martyrdom in the name of Christ."

That his call to ministry didn't necessarily entail a call to comfortable Western Anglican Christianity had simply never before crossed Michael's mind. *Here I am, dressed up in fancy vestments in this ornate chapel,* he told himself, *thinking I'm going to go out from here and play at church!*

It was a life-altering moment for Michael. From the time he'd arrived at Nashotah House, God had been shaking him and shaping him, pounding home lessons in humility and obedience, in giving up his own willfulness, ambitions, and desires. This simple account of martyrdom had now brought him to rock bottom.

Right then and there, Michael made a vow to God that he would never ever play at church. Maybe he didn't quite know yet what being a priest meant or what he'd be doing in ministry. But from this point on, he would commit himself to being deadly serious about his faith and to never allow his life to dishonor the sacrifices others were making to serve Christ. That determination in that moment became the foundation upon which he would build his concept of ministry.

And that commitment would soon be sorely tested. In Michael's senior year of seminary, after enduring several difficult miscarriages,

Aimee was once again pregnant. Their daughter, Hadley Laud, was born in March 2007, just two months before Michael's graduation.

By this point, the news of a church split back in Michael's home diocese of Tennessee had been made public. The bishop who had first approved Michael's appointment to seminary, Bertram Herlong, had recently retired, and a new bishop, John Bauerschmidt, had taken over the Tennessee diocese. Since the split, Bishop Herlong had been filling in at All Saints until a full-time minister could be appointed.

That's where they're going to send me after graduation, immediately crossed Michael's mind. He dismissed the thought just as quickly. With the bitter nature of the church split, serving at All Saints would be a spiritual minefield—the diocese would surely appoint a far more experienced hand to take over. But when Michael flew down to Nashville to meet with Bishop John Bauerschmidt about his first assignment, he was somehow not surprised when the bishop told him, "I'd like to send you to All Saints in Smyrna."

"I just knew you were going to say that," Michael managed to respond calmly. "Can you give me the lay of the land there?"

"Well, there's only about twenty-five people left in the congregation. The mortgage is $850,000, with interest payments alone running about $5,500 a month. All Saints has been designated a mission church, since it's no longer self-supporting, so the diocese will cover your stipend for now. The diocese has given All Saints $10,000 to get things started again."

Ten thousand dollars. While a generous gesture, that wasn't even two months' mortgage payments. This was hardly the first assignment Michael had anticipated. "I need to talk to Aimee and think and pray on this first. What if I don't accept the position? What are my other options?"

"I don't know," the bishop replied simply. "But I want you to talk with Aimee, take a look, and let me know what you think."

Climbing into his rental car, Michael began the drive from Nashville down to Smyrna some twenty miles further south. While he drove, he called Aimee to fill her in on the bishop's news. But just a few minutes into the conversation, Michael caught himself. *What am I doing?*

This was exactly the attitude he'd displayed to Father Bill all those years ago. The very same argument he'd made to Bishop Herlong about the assignment to Nashotah House. As to the overwhelming burden of mortgage and other church expenses, had he forgotten how God had supplied again and again during his seminary years?

Have I learned nothing about trusting God and obedience to his will? I need to obey my bishop and accept this assignment. Ending his phone call with Aimee, Michael called the bishop back. "I don't know what I was thinking. Of course I accept."

By the time Michael reached All Saints, walked around the redbrick building, and stood on the green knoll, looking out over fields, trees, and creek, he had no further doubts. Flying back to Wisconsin, he described for Aimee the small English-village-style church and the absolute peace and certainty he'd felt there.

Aimee found the news disheartening at first. Michael's other classmates had all been appointed to thriving parishes or academic positions. They'd all be working under experienced superiors. In contrast, the All Saints appointment meant Michael would be working alone. The news that the church was close to shutting its doors was even more discouraging. But she voiced none of these concerns, instead offering immediate support to Michael's eagerness.

Two months later, graduation over, the Spurlocks moved into their new home in Murfreesboro, Tennessee, just a few miles from Smyrna, and Michael began his service at All Saints.

13

And indeed All Saints became home as much as Nashotah House had been. Whatever the drawbacks, Michael discovered that the role of a parish vicar was made for him. He loved leading services in the simple white-walled sanctuary with its soaring, stained-wood ceiling and beautifully carved altar. Studying God's Word, then teaching it to his congregation, was a joy. The simple services, accompanied by the small organ and the few voices singing the hymns, might not compare to the soaring harmonies and liturgy of Nashville's cathedral or Nashotah's chapel, but the worship was sincere and rooted in the love of Jesus.

The congregation too had proved friendly enough and eager to meet their new vicar. Some had teased, "You've no idea what you're in for! What did you do to the bishop to deserve this?"

But for the most part, All Saints' small congregation simply wanted to get on with the business of healing and rebuilding a once thriving church. They each had a painful story to tell, and Michael took time to listen, reliving the church split from many different perspectives. Having never been in charge of a parish, Michael encountered daily some new task he'd never done before, from counseling to heading up hospital visitation.

While Michael was acquiring his sea legs as vicar, Aimee too was finding her place. Cooking meals, planning family times, caring for Atticus and Hadley were all a welcome hiatus from the busy professional life she'd known. Her "nesting time" was how she thought of it. She also began leading a youth choir at St. Paul's, a large Episcopal church near their home in Murfreesboro.

Above all, she loved seeing her husband flourish in his new vocation. One of her journal entries in January 2008 rejoiced: "Michael's sermon today was fantastic. He's so talented. We had five new people today. I was so excited and thrilled to think that these people could become part of our community and at the same time have a closer relationship to Christ."

But while Aimee didn't miss the frantic pace of New York City, she did miss the affirmation and challenge of her professional life. It wasn't so long ago she'd been singing such operatic roles as *Faust*'s Marguerite, Micaela in *Carmen*, Musetta in *La Bohème*. Or interviewing Hollywood stars at the Oscars. While she loved her husband and completely supported his calling to serve God, at times she felt lost in the shuffle.

Aimee was helping her precocious firstborn with homework one day when he raised the topic of what she'd done for a living before his birth. Only half-joking, she told him, "I used to be somebody."

His expressive, dark eyes opening wide, Atticus reassured Aimee earnestly, "Mommy, you *are* somebody."

It didn't help that Aimee's multiple sclerosis had flared up after Hadley's birth, so that she was again struggling with the same exhaustion and pain she'd dealt with after the birth of Atticus. Then there were her worries about her husband and the goals and expectations facing them at All Saints. Despite all Michael's talent and hard work, there was no denying that things were not progressing as well or as quickly as Aimee, Michael, or the diocese had hoped.

One older woman in particular tried all of Aimee's Christian patience. A minister's widow, she was accustomed to holding the reins at All Saints. The "lay pope" of All Saints, Aimee had heard her called when they first arrived. Aimee ignored the constant digs at her "deficiencies" as a vicar's wife. But one day she walked into church with a new haircut.

As Aimee entered the sanctuary, the woman looked her up and down. Then with the honeyed, smiling drawl that could be a southern woman's most vicious weapon, she asked Aimee, "Did you *mean* to do that to your hair?"

On another occasion, she told Aimee with a saccharine smile, "Honey, if Michael were just a couple years older and I a couple years younger, you'd be in trouble, because I'd take your husband right out from under your nose."

Michael was having his own problems with the woman, who handled much of the church's financial affairs. Michael's position as vicar didn't impress her in the slightest. After one acerbic discussion over some expenditure she objected to, she snapped at Michael, "Look, buster, the honeymoon's over!"

To Michael, the honeymoon had been over for some time. As he'd anticipated, the biggest issue was the church's financial situation. Though Michael was All Saints' spiritual leader, the church council managed its financial affairs. By this time, Michael had gained a fair handle on the situation. Beyond his own salary, the diocese had for the time being committed $1,500 a month to All Saints as a mission outreach. Church offerings were averaging $3,000 a month. Not enough to cover the minimum mortgage payment of $5,500 along with utilities, church upkeep, and other incidentals. Which meant drawing a little further each month on that $10,000 seed money the diocese had contributed when they'd appointed Michael to All Saints.

Neither Michael, the diocesan leadership, nor the remaining congregants wanted to see the doors of All Saints close. Smyrna was a growing area that had become a commuting suburb to Nashville. There was ample potential here for a church plant like All Saints. But by September 2007, three months after the Spurlocks had arrived, the math could not be denied. According to current giving patterns, All Saints would be completely broke by the end of the year. Especially since the original split, just ten months earlier, had been ugly enough that few families searching for a new church home bothered to visit All Saints.

More pertinently, the enormous debt was such a drain on the congregation's emotional energy, resources, and anxieties that the only real mission each month had become how to make that mortgage payment. The only logical way to free the congregation from this burden so they could move forward with a new vision and mission was to sell the church building and its outlying property. Of the twenty-two acres the church owned, seventeen were bottomland sitting in a floodplain. It had once been farmed but could not be zoned for development. Still, the entire property was now worth more than when it was purchased, so by selling it, the congregation could pay off the mortgage and have some profit with which to make a new start.

None of this was new to the congregation or church council. After all, they'd been wrestling with the problem since the past November, long before Michael arrived on the scene. First with the church council, then at a congregational meeting, Michael set up a whiteboard and went through the numbers. Reluctantly, but unanimously, the council and congregation agreed that the only viable option was to approach the diocese and formally ask for permission to put the church property up for sale. For Michael, it was a great burden removed from his shoulders. The decision had been a hard one, but at least the church body was now all of one mind.

Or so Michael thought. Only after the congregation had ratified the Mission Council's vote did Michael learn that one church council member had initiated his own personal campaign to oppose the sale. When Michael reminded him at the next council meeting that he had helped develop the plan to sell the church and voted for it, he turned on Michael in a rage. Who was Michael, a complete outsider and stranger, to come into their town and their church and destroy what they had worked so hard to build? Threatening Michael with a beating and calling him a stream of vile names, he stormed out of the meeting.

Though it was late in the evening, Michael drove to the council member's house to attempt reconciliation. After all, he could sympathize with the man's hurt and frustration over losing the church he'd worked so hard to build. More so, this man was among those who'd stayed when most of the congregation had abandoned All Saints. Selling out would be a galling admission of defeat to all those who'd left. Michael expressed his understanding, explained again the hard realities behind the council's decision, and shared his own commitment to All Saints and vision for rebuilding. With a hug and warm handshake, he took his leave, thinking they'd reached an agreement.

Then Michael discovered that far from agreement, the man had begun repeatedly calling church families, trying to convince them that Michael was an outsider who could not be trusted and that the vote was a mistake that needed rescinding. At wits' end, Michael called Bishop Bauerschmidt and explained the situation.

The bishop's response was immediate and uncompromising. "There's nothing about your vocation that requires you to take malicious abuse. The church council serves the parish under the spiritual authority of the bishop and vicar, not the other way around. I'm afraid you're going to have to rescind this person's appointment to the council, and you have my full support in doing so."

With regret, Michael wrote a letter rescinding the council member's appointment. The man immediately left the church and never attended again. Michael had been vicar for only a few months, and to him, this seemed a failure on his part to hold things together. He hoped this wouldn't be the pattern of his ministry at All Saints.

14

At least the remaining congregation was now unified behind the sale. The next step was an appraisal and inspection of the building. The inspection was necessary because, ironically, the church's concrete foundation had split right down the middle from one end of the building to other. Until the church was certified in sound condition, it could not be put on the market.

It was October 2007. The council expected the building would go on the market by the end of the month and that the All Saints congregation would be moved out by Christmas. But one obstacle after another delayed the inspection, and Michael celebrated his first Christmas as a priest in All Saints' beautiful sanctuary. For this very first Christmas Eve service, he wanted every detail to be perfect. They would have "smells and bells," as Aimee termed it.

Atticus was now eight years old and excited to be serving as an acolyte for the very first time. Part of the liturgy for the service included the use of incense burned in a censer suspended on chains. The gentle swinging of the censer resulted in an aromatic smoke symbolizing the prayers of God's people rising to God's throne.

Holding nine-month-old Hadley in a baby sling, Aimee watched as her husband, son, and the rest of the procession threaded down the sanctuary aisle. The thurifer, whose assignment it was to swing the censer, had been heavy-handed with the incense so that the smoke now filling the church was proving too much for even

Michael's comfort. Michael stepped through the haze to begin his sermon.

That was when Aimee noticed the fixed expression and green tinge on her firstborn's face. Atticus had just returned from a week's stay with his great-grandfather, where he'd thoroughly enjoyed being spoiled with Pepsi, Coke, and other rich, sugary treats he wasn't accustomed to at home. Clearly, the heavy smoke and his sugar withdrawal were not proving a good combination. That midnight was long past his bedtime didn't help. Atticus half-walked, half-ran out of the sanctuary. Concerned, Aimee followed.

Just as she stepped outside, the fire alarm went off. Aimee found her firstborn throwing up in the grass to the blare of the alarm. Hadley chose that moment to add her own screams to the commotion. Before Aimee could calm either child, she heard Michael calling urgently, "Babe?"

Turning, Aimee saw her husband poke his head out the church door. Why wasn't he inside preaching his sermon? "Babe, I keep punching in the code, but the alarm won't stop going off. Can you do something about the sound? Take the batteries out or something?"

In full confidence of his wife's capabilities, Michael ran back in to continue the service. Rounding up one nauseous and one hysterical offspring, Aimee hurried in to deal with the alarm. She found some old kneeling cushions and packing tape. Stuffing the cushions over the siren, she began plastering packing tape to hold them to the wall.

Though the alarm was still sounding, it was at least muffled enough to complete the service in relative peace. But it was hardly the image of perfection both Michael and Aimee had hoped for. Aimee could either laugh or cry over the evening's ruined expectations. She chose to laugh. Gathering up her exhausted children and waiting for Michael to greet the people and change out of his vestments, Aimee gave a humorous mental shrug. *Well, so much for the perfect vicar's family! Who says God doesn't have a sense of humor!*

Christmas over, church focus returned to the property sale. Despite continued sadness over the decision to sell, Michael and the congregation were seeing God answer one prayer after another. The inspection finally happened, and the foundation and building were declared sound. They were now waiting on the appraiser who had been appointed by the diocese. Once again, delay after delay in finishing the appraisal prevented the property from being put on the market.

It was then that Michael became witness to an ongoing miracle. According to all calculations, the church's $10,000 financial cushion should have been long spent by now. But like the Old Testament miracle of a godly widow and her never-emptying barrel of meal and cruse of oil (1 Kings 17), the church's bank account balance never seemed to get lower. First, a few new families pushed the offering higher than calculated. Then a drop in interest rates lowered the monthly mortgage payment. If there was never extra, there was always just enough to pay one more month's bills.

By the time All Saints was finally listed for sale, Easter was right around the corner. It was a surprise to be celebrating Holy Week and Easter still in their own facility. The services were reverent and worked to inspire the close to fifty parishioners who regularly attended, and the scores of visitors who swelled the congregation at Easter. Michael found himself battling to ignore the beauty and serenity of this place. He steadfastly resisted walking down the hill to enjoy the twenty-two acres of meadow, creek, and trees. Getting emotionally attached would just make it that much harder to leave.

In truth, both Michael and the rest of the congregation were becoming anxious to get it over with and to be able to move on to whatever the future held.

Then the purchase offer came.

And the arrival at Sunday morning worship of three strangers from a people group and war zone on the far side of the planet of whose very existence Michael had never even heard.

❄ ❄ ❄

Establishing a Karen home-in-exile in a small town of central Tennessee was hardly the result of intentional planning. At least by any *human* agency.

Stepping off the plane in North Carolina, Ye Win did not doubt God had opened this door. But his early months in a vast, new country called America were as bewildering as they were frustrating. A southern drawl was not the English dialect he'd learned to understand or speak. Just walking into a grocery store or Walmart left one paralyzed with the choices.

And so much paper work just to function! Immigration documents. Driver's license. Medical insurance. Social Security card. Green card.

Worse, even as a rebel fighter or a political activist, Ye Win had been part of a community. Here, he and his new wife were outsiders and alone. Volunteers with the refugee settlement agency were friendly, but they soon had new clients to deal with.

Ye Win coped by pursuing even more paper work. He began tracking down his siblings and remaining family in Myanmar. By then, one brother and sister had joined his uncle, Ye Ga My, in Australia. His parents were still in Myanmar, where his mother taught school and his father continued as an itinerant evangelist. His youngest sister, Khin Kyi, was a first-year law student in Rangoon. Their situation was growing more precarious the longer they stayed in Myanmar. The Burmese military were not convinced John and Daisy Kunoo maintained no contact with Ye Win or their other revolutionary offspring. Routinely, officials showed up at their house, demanding information as well as their cut of the money the Kunoos must surely receive from family overseas. It was time for Ye Win's parents and youngest sister to join the rest of the family in exile.

While Ye Win could not contact his parents directly, one uncle still served as an Anglican missionary in Myanmar. He in turn was in contact with a fellow Anglican priest, Father Bu Christ, currently rector of a church in Mae La, Thailand's largest refugee camp. Through this circuitous route, Ye Win made contact with his parents, who agreed it was time to leave. Ye Win then sent funds to the refugee camp to provide passage across the border for his parents and sister.

Meanwhile, in Rangoon, Ye Win's sister, Khin Kyi, received an unexpected phone call from her parents. No explanation, just a request that she leave law school immediately and return home. Though bewildered, Khin Kyi was on the bus the next day, leaving all her personal belongings behind. When she arrived home, her parents informed her, "We're leaving the country tomorrow morning."

And indeed, the next morning all three were on a bus heading east. At each city in which the bus stopped, they had to show ID and explain their travel. Their pretext was visiting friends. Once they crossed over into Karen territory, Ye Win's missionary uncle and the funds he'd sent played their role. Paid-off checkpoint and border guards looked the other way as a vehicle carrying the Kunoo family crossed into Thailand. They would remain in the Mae La refugee camp for two years until refugee visas finally came through for them to join Ye Win in the United States.

By this time Ye Win had also moved again. Two Karen families had already settled in Smyrna, Tennessee, including a friend who invited Ye Win to join them. Ye Win's parents and sister arrived in Smyrna in 2007. But they were not alone. They had traveled as part of a larger group from Father Bu Christ's refugee camp church, a total of five families along with single adults. A house church was born, with Father Bu Christ leading services in living rooms and backyard green spaces. When other Karen heard of the Smyrna nucleus, they asked to come as well. Soon, the initial two families had grown to more than a hundred.

Ye Win now had his community. He had kept his vow to serve God and his people. But the resultant workload soon overwhelmed him. Refugee benefits paid rent for only three months. And Rutherford County, where Smyrna was located, had no refugee settlement agency such as had placed Ye Win and his wife in North Carolina. Refugee families choosing to settle there were on their own. And unlike Ye Win's own family, most of the other Karen refugees had spent the last generation in the jungle or refugee camps. Few had more than minimal education, and even fewer spoke any English. Ye Win also had the only driver's license and vehicle.

So it was left to Ye Win to pick up new families at the airport. To find them a place to live and a steady job. To help them fill out government forms for Social Security cards, food stamps, Medicaid, Section Eight. To enroll their children in school. To drive them to OB-GYN and other doctor's appointments.

And, of course, to church.

15

By the following Sunday, All Saints' original Anglo congregation could no longer ignore the changes to their quiet, calm, and *empty* country church. But if some were appalled at being suddenly outnumbered by Southeast Asian immigrants and their restless offspring, others felt very differently.

Mark and Landra Orr had been part of the All Saints church plant since its storefront inception. They'd worked and organized and sacrificed financially to build the current sanctuary. Their children had grown up in its Sunday school and youth group.

The Karen people weren't new to them. The Orrs had actually been part of a World Relief project to sponsor the first Karen refugee family in Smyrna. They'd waved welcome signs at the airport when the family arrived. A professional social worker, Landra had helped them find housing, transportation, jobs. The Orrs had even transported that family, along with some non-Karen Burmese refugees, to services at All Saints, then a packed-out, growing church.

Then came the split. The handful of refugees had disappeared with the rest of the congregation. The Orrs made a commitment to stay. But to Landra, the trauma went far deeper than a congregational disagreement. She had poured her life, her heart, into All Saints, and now it felt as though her own family had cast her out and turned their backs on her. There was no more socializing with old friends, not even talking when they ran into each other around town. Worse was the conflict's devastating impact on her own teenage children, who no longer wanted anything to do with church.

Father Michael Spurlock's arrival had restored hope for All Saints' future. Landra had been part of the church council, brainstorming fundraisers, grants, and other ideas to keep the church property afloat. In the end, all to no avail.

Now Landra took note of disapproving frowns from certain proper southern ladies sitting nearby. Her social worker's eye noted the undisciplined juvenile behavior and other ecclesiastical infractions from their visitors. But, like Michael, she did not see chaos but a sanctuary that was once again full. A fresh wind had just blown new life into All Saints. What it might entail for their small congregation, she had no idea. But she at least had a genuine smile for the newcomers as she stepped forward to greet them.

❅ ❅ ❅

Michael Williams too had straightened up with excitement when he first saw the Karen parading into the sanctuary. Once a Methodist pastor, Michael had received his doctorate in pastoral theology at St. Mary's Graduate School of Theology in Cleveland, Ohio, then gone on to teach homiletics there. After retiring in 2004, he acceded to his wife Judy's pleas to find a warmer climate. The couple had moved to Smyrna in 2007. They'd grown accustomed to a liturgical service at St. Mary's, so All Saints was among the first churches they'd visited. On that first visit, Michael counted only twelve others in attendance. During the coffee hour after the service, one member approached the couple.

"You probably don't want to start attending here," Michael and Judy were told. "This church is about to close. We've got a million-dollar debt and will be selling this property to pay it off."

If intended to discourage, the words had an opposite effect on Michael. This was clearly a church with a need, and perhaps God was calling him to this new mission. The Williamses came back the next Sunday. It was the first Sunday for the church's new vicar, a fresh young seminary graduate named Father Michael Spurlock.

The Williamses were impressed enough to look no further for a home church.

But one thing Michael Williams missed in their move south was being part of a multicultural church. Michael had always felt strongly about racial division, especially within the church. In fact, a young Michael had been among white participants in the 1965 Selma civil rights march with Dr. Martin Luther King. The arrival of seventy Karen into their tiny Caucasian conclave was to Michael simply a confirmation that this was a mission to which God had called him.

※ ※ ※

Merry Adams had actually been the first to take note of Ye Win and his family on their first visit, since her wheelchair sat at the left rear of the sanctuary just inside the door. Born on Christmas Day 1954 in Orlando, Florida, Merry had been among the first generation of children to receive the polio vaccine. When two weeks of fever left seven-year-old Merry with vomiting, severe joint pain, and paralysis, the family doctor insisted Merry's symptoms had to be psychosomatic. It took a year to find a doctor who correctly diagnosed Merry's condition as the aftermath of the polio vaccine. By then Merry's right leg was virtually useless. She would spend the rest of her life using braces, crutches, and eventually a wheelchair.

Merry's parents were far from wealthy and had three other children. But they did everything in their power to seek therapy for Merry, their firstborn, eventually getting her into a school for children with mobile disabilities. There Merry acquired a love of reading, books providing an escape into worlds beyond the limited range of her wheelchair. Her parents treated Merry no differently than her younger siblings, offering the same love, support, and discipline. That included chores. Merry learned to make her bed, clean her room, and do the dishes, all from a seated position.

But the church their family had faithfully attended proved less kind. Their particular denominational doctrine taught that illness resulted from sin, either Merry's parents' or her own. It annoyed

Merry when church women would pat her on the head and tell her how sweet and brave she was. But she was even more infuriated when she overheard some of the same women speculating over what sin her daddy must have committed to cause Merry's illness.

Merry herself was treated as though her disability were contagious. She would never forget an early incident. Though Merry now had a wheelchair, the church was not equipped for handicapped access, so her father would carry Merry to the second floor, where children's classes were held. Setting her in a chair among the other children, he would then head downstairs to his own class.

One Sunday, a teacher walked in, spotted Merry, and ordered the children into the next room. Since Merry couldn't move, she assumed the teacher would return for her. But soon she heard the children laughing and singing in the usual Sunday school format. First puzzled, Merry grew increasingly scared. Only when her father returned for her after class did Merry learn that the teacher had deliberately abandoned her for fear of contamination. Eventually the family stopped attending church. Merry assumed it was her fault because of her polio. Years later, her father explained it hadn't been Merry's fault, but the hypocrisy they'd witnessed.

The family moved to Tennessee in Merry's junior year of high school. Merry went on to graduate from college, but didn't return to church until age twenty-four, when she was hired as a part-time secretary by an Episcopal parish in Murfreesboro. She'd never abandoned her faith in God, only the church, and curiosity drew her to attend services. Over the next years, she drifted from Tennessee to Alabama, then back, and in and out of several churches. But something was missing.

What she needed was community, Merry decided. What would it be like to be part of some small town where you could go into the local grocery store and greet people who knew you from church? Maybe that would fill the empty hole in her heart. *If I could find a church that really acted like Jesus, and where people were accepted regardless of appearance, disabilities, or skin color, I would go!*

In the meantime, sleeping in and reading the Sunday paper in bed was more attractive than going to church. Merry had also found herself in a string of bad relationships. She finally decided to stop dating until she got her life straightened out. With that in mind, she began investigating metaphysics, astrology, New Age, and other philosophies. But however mixed-up her religious life, Merry realized she just couldn't give up Jesus. Despite negative church experiences, her childhood faith was too ingrained.

Then in 1993, Merry met a navy veteran named Paul Adams who loved books as much as she did. Six months later, they were married. In 2000, the Adamses moved to Smyrna. Like Merry, Paul was a lapsed churchgoer. Sunday was their day of leisure. But for Merry, something still felt missing. She'd been aware of Smyrna's new Episcopal church as well as its exceedingly acrimonious split. Then one day she saw in the newspaper that All Saints had a new vicar.

"I want to go back to church," she told Paul.

"Fine with me so long as you don't expect me to go" was his laconic response.

In Father Michael and Aimee Spurlock, Merry found the welcome she'd been searching for. She'd been attending less than a month when she saw a group of dark-haired, brown-skinned strangers enter past her wheelchair. Whether they were Hispanic, Native American, or some other ethnicity, it didn't matter. She'd prayed for a church that made all comers welcome. Now the onus was on her to help make that a reality at All Saints.

❋ ❋ ❋

Aimee's hospitable soul felt nothing but delight to see their visitors back. She greeted adults, herded children from danger zones, made sure additional packages of cookies and pitchers of Kool-Aid were available. By the end of the after-service coffee hour, every morsel of food and drink had been devoured, crumbs were everywhere, and the entire building was in disarray.

Father Michael Spurlock was no less excited about how God had answered their prayers. *My church is full! Whatever else, it is full!*

Part of the All Saints congregation when Michael Spurlock arrived (from left to right): Shirley Hutson, the Reverend Tom Hutson, Kathy Short, Merry Adams, Bo Ezell, Paul Adams, Mark Orr, Michael Williams, Landra Orr

Michael Spurlock is currently Curate and Associate for Pastoral Care at St. Thomas Church Fifth Avenue in New York City. To this day, he is close with the people of All Saints.

Reverend Michael Spurlock with John Corbett, who plays the role of Spurlock in the film, on the set of *All Saints*

Michael (Corbett) and a member of the congregation (Barry Corbin) discussing challenges that lie ahead

Atticus Spurlock (Myles Moore) and Po Win (played by
Ye Win's son John Wise Win) form a new friendship

Michael (Corbett)
ponders the future
of All Saints

Michael (Corbett) is filmed welcoming the Karen refugees to All Saints

Michael (Corbett), Ye Win (Nelson Lee), and the All Saints congregation before they plant the seeds for the farm behind All Saints church

Cast of *All Saints* in front of All Saints church, including the real-life Karen church members who played themselves in the film

Michael (Corbett) and Aimee (Cara Buono) discuss their family's needs

Michael (Corbett) harvesting crops

Michael (Corbett) and Aimee (Buono) teach children at All Saints

Reverend Michael Spurlock and Ye Win. It all started with "Hello."

Ye Win remains All Saints' lay worker, tending to the needs of its ever-growing Karen refugee community. He is happily married with four children.

The Spurlock family today: Michael, Atticus, Aimee, and Hadley

All Saints membership today in front of their church, where the movie was actually filmed

16

M ichael had become cognizant of just how much work
lay ahead. Ye Win, in turn, had not forgotten his
intention to continue Michael's education. Gradually, Michael learned not only the current situation of Smyrna's
refugee population but also the personal life stories of his new
congregants, including Father Thomas Bu Christ.

Since arriving in the United States, Thomas Bu Christ had not
been able to find work due to a serious back injury. His wife, Hae
Htoo Pi, a trained nurse and teacher in her own country, had been
forced to become the breadwinner, supporting their family of five
on a minimum wage job. But Michael was amazed and humbled
to discover that the short, stocky older Karen, who insisted on
addressing him with such deference, had in his own country and
the Thai refugee camps overseen a large Anglican congregation as
well as a Christian school. He was, in fact, a far more experienced
ministry leader than Michael.

Taking mental note to check into certifying Father Bu Christ
as an ordained minister in Tennessee, Michael queried, "What
about the rest of your community? What type of jobs did they
hold back in Myanmar?"

Not all the Karen refugees were educated professionals like the
Kunoos, Father Bu Christ, or Christ Paw, Ye Win explained. Most
had been rural farmers before the Burmese military had burned

their villages and driven them from their land. Unfortunately, this had not proved a marketable job skill in Smyrna.

Ye Win went on to explain that he'd found housing for a large portion of the Karen community at a nearby housing development, Chalet Apartments, just two miles from the church. That at least explained how so many had arrived on foot.

He'd also scraped up unskilled menial jobs for several dozen Karen at a Tyson chicken processing plant as well as Nashville's Pro-Cut industrial complex, where Ye Win himself worked as a machine operator. But a lack of reliable transportation was jeopardizing these jobs. And with benefits running out, sufficient food for what tended to be large and growing families was becoming an issue, along with such basics as clothing, household furnishings, and school supplies.

But though Michael braced himself to explain again that their small congregation could hardly meet all these needs, the Karen delegation's requests were in the end modest. Their homes were too small to hold church services for their growing community. Would Father Michael permit them to hold their Sunday worship at All Saints after the Anglo congregation had finished?

"I'll have to get the bishop's approval, but that shouldn't be a problem," Michael immediately agreed.

"And we also wondered . . ." There was clear hesitation and a murmur among the delegation in Karen before Ye Win finished. "We see the church has much land that is not in use. If our people could plant gardens, it would provide food for those who are going without."

This should have been an even simpler request. But Michael fell silent. The land was certainly available. But how could he encourage these people to plant gardens when any day this property might no longer belong to All Saints?

Perhaps more pertinently, the previous vicar had made a trade with Smyrna's department of parks and recreation to use All Saints' surplus bottomland for multiple practice softball fields in exchange for cutting the grass. The idea had been that the exchange would garner some community goodwill and perhaps some membership. The city had invested money grading much of the church's twenty-two acres and sowing it with Bermuda grass to create a smooth, green lawn suitable for sports. They would not be happy to see refugees tearing up their lawn for food crops.

After a pause, Michael said slowly, "So long as you don't touch the softball fields, you are welcome to plant anything you like. And you are welcome to hold services here as long as we are in this building. But I've already explained the situation with the property sale. I can't guarantee we'll still be here by the time your gardens would be ready to harvest."

"We understand," Ye Win said quietly, the others nodding agreement as Ye Win translated Michael's response.

The changes didn't take long to implement. Michael's own presence at All Saints was an indicator of Bishop Bauerschmidt's heart for any mission endeavor, and as Michael had anticipated, he gave immediate approval. The church council raised no objection either. After all, it wouldn't be for long with the church sale right around the corner. The very next Sunday, the Karen began arriving at All Saints as the Anglo congregation filed out.

Within the month, sharing the church between two congregations had become routine. Michael would stay after the Anglo service to help the Karen access everything necessary for their own service and Eucharist. Occasionally, he would stay for their service while Aimee and the children headed home.

Michael also cleared out a room just inside the back door of the church for storing donations. A food and clothing drive soon filled it, and Ye Win was appointed to oversee distribution. Far more Karen were in need than those attending All Saints, Ye Win explained. Many refugees were not even Christian, but Buddhists or animists. Others were Christian, but attending another Anglo church or not attending church at all in this country. The aid was shared according to need, regardless of church or religious affiliation.

Though always willing to lend a hand or surreptitiously add a few extra twenty-pound bags of rice to the storage room, Michael was too busy to more than touch base in passing with the newcomers. After all, he had an entire parish to care for, not just the Karen.

So there was far more that Michael did not learn until much later. That working what was essentially two full-time jobs was placing a serious strain on Ye Win's own family life. That Ye Win was maxing out his own credit cards to help other Karen meet their bills. That flying cross-country to help drive another Karen family to Smyrna had come close to costing him his own job.

Or that the same anonymous troublemakers who had informed the Karen that All Saints' remaining congregation were apostates who didn't believe in Jesus had also told them that if they began attending All Saints, they would receive no help there, nor any further assistance from other charitable groups currently helping them. He learned too what had instigated the Kunoo family's first visit. When their bishop back in Myanmar had assured the Karen that the Episcopalian church was America's Anglican counterpart, the group had elected Ye Win and his family to discreetly check out All Saints on their behalf.

All this Michael pieced together only in bits and pieces as Ye Win acted as a liaison and interpreter to the much larger group now sharing their church building. Aware of several vocal Anglo members who were unhappy at the influx, Michael did his best to ensure his original congregation was not unduly inconvenienced. But to his surprise, a number expressed disappointment that the Karen were no longer attending the morning service. Then Ye Win shared that the Karen were voicing a similar dissatisfaction. If they were one body in Christ, why were they not worshiping their heavenly Father together? Maybe they could reinstitute it for special occasions at least?

"I agree," Michael responded to both groups. "So long as Father Bu Christ shares in the services with me."

By early May, the two congregations had become one. The merger was not without its hiccups. The Karen children were still not accustomed to sitting quietly on wooden benches instead of running around mats on the floor. There were times when an escaped child would dash up front to stand beside Michael as he preached or administered the Eucharist. The Anglo congregants found this either adorable or infuriating.

Then there was the ringing of unsilenced cell phones. The whispering back and forth as those visitors who understood English explained the service to those who didn't. Which was most of the Karen. When Father Bu Christ took a turn, the Anglo congregation grumbled in turn that it was meaningless babble.

"Now you understand how they feel listening to our service," Michael reminded his Anglo members sternly. "It will be good for us to take our turn."

But the two groups came together when singing familiar hymns and reading from *The Book of Common Prayer*, each in their own language. And the beautiful symbolism of the Eucharist, with Father Bu Christ administering host and cup to kneeling communicants on one side of the carved-wood railing and Father Michael on the other, needed no translation. Contact with the Archbishop of Myanmar during a global Anglican Church leadership conference confirmed that Father Bu Christ was indeed an Anglican priest in good standing, so he'd been approved to serve as such within the Tennessee diocese.

In fact, within a few weeks, Michael had begun to ponder if there was some way to keep their blended congregation together even once All Saints lost their building. He'd also approached the diocese to see if they might come up with a stipend for Father Bu Christ as a fellow priest. But that idea was quickly shot down since Michael's own salary was already a stretch of diocesan funds.

Ye Win had not yet followed through with his proposal to plant gardens. But sitting alone in his church office, Michael was surprised to see Karen walking along the fence dividing church land from the highway, pulling up what appeared to be weeds. They did the same along the creek and tree line that edged the church's bottomland. Michael learned that they were actually harvesting edible greens. When spring rains brought the usual wild onions springing up all over the lawn, he saw Karen women and children carefully pulling up every shoot.

One day Michael spotted a snapping turtle laying eggs down near the creek. Thinking the Karen might find it an interesting novelty, he called several nearby to take a look. One immediately snatched up the turtle, while others gathered the eggs. A stunned Michael finally registered that they'd assumed he was offering them a free meal.

These people are survivors! Michael realized. *I look out over our land and see weeds and wildlife. They see dinner!*

17

One principle Michael had set from the Karen's first arrival at All Saints was that the church would not just be running a handout ministry. For one, their tiny congregation didn't have those kinds of resources. But the principle also reflected Michael's fundamental beliefs on how to help others. "Give a man a fish, and you've fed him for a day; teach a man to fish, and he can feed himself for a lifetime" might be an overworked cliché, but it held truth. Michael believed strongly that the most effective giving came from building relationships, and through that, an understanding of what the real needs were. Welcoming these newcomers into the church as equals, getting to know them personally, investing time and energy to teach how to "fish" took priority over simply writing a check or handing out sacks of rice.

In this case, learning to fish included learning to survive in American culture. Landra Orr and another church member, Kathy Short, were already volunteering with some needed health care. Merry Adams had once worked as a legal aid and offered her services for negotiating bureaucracies such as family services and school registrations. Michael Williams, whose long experience had led to his appointment as Father Michael's pastoral assistant, was willing to tutor children in their homework and pitch in with driving.

But an urgent need for all the Karen was to learn basic English, and Michael had an idea for that. He'd finally met Merry Adams' husband, Paul. Not because Paul had relented about church attendance, but because Paul was trying to stop smoking. Side effects from his Chantix prescription were driving him crazy, and counseling had been recommended. Michael had agreed to see him informally during the week, and within a few sessions they'd developed a good relationship. Paul had let slip that he'd taught English as a Second Language (ESL) classes in the past. To Michael, it was a banner-waving sign direct from heaven.

Thank you, God, for sending this man to my office, he prayed silently. But before Michael could bring the conversation around to his proposal, Paul was leaning forward. "Hey, you look like something is really bothering you."

"Well, yes," Michael admitted. "I don't know how much Merry has told you. But we have this group of refugees who want to be part of our church. You're not likely to have heard of them. I certainly hadn't. But they are called the Karen."

But Paul's expression showed no sign of Michael's own earlier incomprehension. "Of course I've heard of them. You're talking about the tribal group from Myanmar, formerly Burma."

Michael's own raised eyebrows displayed his surprise. "Wow, you're the first person I've met around here who knows who they are. I'm trying to see what I can do for them. I'd really like to set up some basic volunteer services."

Michael took a deep breath before launching into his proposal. "Paul, I believe God has brought you here for a reason. And that reason is to start an English program."

"You mean, like ESL classes?" Paul answered.

"Yes, like you said you used to teach. I want you to run the program."

This time it was Paul's eyebrows that shot high. "Whoa! I can't teach a class for your church. I'm not even a Christian! You need to find someone who actually attends your church."

Michael leaned forward earnestly. "I'm not asking you to teach Sunday school. I just want you to teach English."

❁ ❁ ❁

Paul Adams found himself conflicted over the request. What few in Smyrna knew about Paul was that he'd actually been raised in a devout Christian home. An accomplished vocalist, he'd sung in church choirs and even had a music scholarship to attend Bible college upon graduating from high school. But 1970 was the height of the Vietnam War, and becoming a soldier sounded more exciting than studying theology. Especially since Paul could admit he'd been drifting away from his faith for some time and was as arrogant, overconfident, and full-of-himself as any eighteen-year-old recruit.

Enlisting in the US Navy, Paul trained as a corpsman (battlefield medic). The marines had no medics of their own but were supplied by the navy, and Paul soon found himself assigned to the Second Marine Battalion, Second Regiment, en route to the Mediterranean for Special Operations training. Paul spent the next twenty-three years in the military, though he never did reach Vietnam. When required to list his religious affiliation, he declared himself an agnostic, though he never actually stopped believing there was some divine Being in charge of this universe, whoever that might be.

Although church attendance was no longer part of his life, Paul believed in giving back, whether donating blood, joining a bone marrow donor bank, or volunteering for community service. He liked teaching and had done a stint while still in the military, teaching adult literacy classes to Asian nationals.

Then at his last duty station in Columbus, Ohio, Paul volunteered to teach ESL for Catholic Refugee Services. Among his students were Khmer from the "killing fields" of Cambodia, Vietnamese, East Germans, Latin Americans, and more. Always a voracious reader, he'd become acquainted with the Karen by reading World War II accounts of Karen guerrilla fighters and jungle nurses who'd helped American and British troops survive the Burmese theater of war.

In 1993, Paul retired from the navy, returning to Tennessee, where his family lived. That same year, he met Merry. Their first conversation lasted sixteen hours. She was the first woman he'd met who owned more books than he did. They even had the same taste in literature. By the time they were married, Paul had found a second career working for Radar Business Systems, then eventually for the IRS. By then Paul and Merry had moved to Smyrna. Merry had found work in IT and as a teacher, but she retired in 2004, when worsening health forced her to give up braces and crutches for a power chair.

Then his wife had inexplicably decided to return to church. For Paul, Sunday mornings were designed for opening a cold Heineken, doing the *New York Times* crossword puzzle, and watching football. He had no objection to Merry attending church so long as she didn't drag him along. Paul might never have set foot in All Saints if his own worsening health hadn't pushed him to quit smoking. The Chantix had given him such mood swings and vivid dreams he'd been at his wits' end. He'd gone to Father Michael because he was too cheap to pay for counseling. And because Father Michael was a good guy and Paul's wife attended his church, the All Saints vicar had in turn agreed to meet with Paul.

So now Paul was in a tight corner. He respected Father Michael and had come to appreciate far more than just those free counseling services. Besides, the project sounded intriguing.

Father Michael's earnest gaze hadn't left Paul's face. His internal debate had clearly lasted less time than Paul had thought. He gave a shrug along with a wry smile. "Sure! Why not?!"

At that moment, Paul Adams would have vehemently denied any possibility that his reluctant assent just might prove to be the first step in a twisting, turning, often surprising, undeniably extraordinary journey that would lead him back to faith and God.

18

Time had run out for All Saints. Pentecost Sunday fell that year on May 11. The morning worship service had been a deeply stirring and inspiring experience for both sides of their blended congregation.

So it was a harsh return to earth as Michael remained behind after the service to receive a new group of visitors. Just the day before, Michael had once again gone over the numbers with Bishop Bauerschmidt. A firm offer had now been made, and it was a fair one. The buyers were actually another new congregation looking to move into a church property they could add onto as their church grew. For two full hours, the bishop and Michael had talked through the situation over and over. Was there any alternative to accepting this offer?

But in the end, the math was what the math was. Michael was forced to agree that there was no choice. The bishop had left him with clear instructions. "You need to work up a budget for what you'll need to replant this church and find a place to go."

The church council had done some sporadic work on the budget, and arrangements had been made for the other church's buying committee to inspect their proposed purchase. All Saints now emptied out, Michael waited for the inspection crew to arrive from their own morning service. This proved to be a group of a dozen or more. They were courteous, and Michael welcomed them warmly.

But as they spread out, looking into cupboards, poking into corners, Michael was surprised to feel a rising flood of annoyance.

He could hear their comments, normal enough for property buyers, but to his ears disparaging. "Wow, look at all this wasted space! . . . They could sure have made better use of this. . . . I can't imagine what we'd do with that!"

Michael had stepped briefly away from his own office. When he returned, there were three women digging through the closet that held vestments and other liturgical accessories. One of them muttered, "Look! This must be all that priest stuff they wear!"

By the time the group left, Michael was well beyond annoyance. He felt hurt, offended, demoralized, and depressed. But mostly, he was just plain furious. *What business is it of theirs how we use our space?*

It suddenly dawned on Michael that his anger flowed from the depth of his hurt. A year ago, accepting this offer would have been no skin off Michael's nose. When he'd come here as a new seminary graduate, it had been in obedience to a challenging and not particularly attractive assignment. And he'd been expecting this day for months. So why did it hurt so much? At what point had All Saints shifted from a simple assignment to "my church"?

Because this really is now my church! This is my congregation. I'm one of them now. I'm not just a priest here. I'm their priest. I love these people. And I don't want to leave this church!

Was this the reason God had permitted the property sale to drag out so long? So that Michael would learn to hurt as much for the loss as his congregation would? To trust God's ultimate plan as his people would have to? Whatever the spiritual lesson involved, it didn't ease the pain. Michael would just have to keep hurting since there appeared to be no other option.

Michael returned to his desk. In front of him was a spreadsheet with all the numbers and figures the church council had put together for their new budget. He had work to do if the congregation was to move. But suddenly he could stay indoors no longer. He needed fresh air to blow away the mental cobwebs, if not the annoyance and anger. Michael headed down the hall and out a back door of the church.

He stood at the top of a knoll. The kind of knoll on which castles had once been built. On the far side of the church, a parking lot swept up to the highway. But from this angle, he might have been looking down on an isolated country dell. The sky overhead was slate gray, signaling a storm rolling in. With spring in full bloom, yellow daffodils and white dandelions dotted the bright green of manicured fields, and the trees edging the creek and property line were a rustle of new leaves.

Since his arrival, Michael had assiduously avoided enjoying this view. But that had clearly not kept him as detached as he'd hoped. On impulse, he headed down the knoll to the left and began a slow trek along the property boundary. The whoosh of vehicles up on the highway gave way to a soughing of wind in the trees and a rush of water in the creek. A strong breeze speckled his face with moisture from the impending rain.

As he walked, Michael lifted his face heavenward and began spilling out his heart in prayer. *God, why did you bring me here? This really hurts! Why did you have to drag it all out so long? Why did you send the Karen here if we're just going to have to leave? What do you want from us? I just wish I knew what to do! Give me wisdom. Show me your plan. Just tell me plain and simple what to do next!*

By now Michael had completed the loop and was heading back toward the church and to his budget. All Saints nestled high above him from this new vantage point, the border fence, pavement, even the rush of vehicles that marked the highway, invisible behind the church's redbrick façade and peaked roof and its Celtic cross. His tired leg muscles were a reminder of how ridiculously over-large, however picturesque, the twenty-two acres Michael had just trekked around were for one small congregation. The seventeen acres that comprised this bottomland he was now trudging across had once actually served a purpose, producing rich food crops instead of sprouting backstops and marked-out softball diamonds.

Michael stopped dead in his tracks. To this point in his life, his mature spiritual journey had been one of devotion, worship, and study. He'd prayed regularly and deeply and had felt what he supposed was God's presence. But at this moment he knew God was speaking to him in a near, new, and powerful way. *I have given you farmland. And I have given you sixty-five farmers from the other side of the world. What don't you understand, Michael? You must start a farm.*

Michael looked around with new interest at the lush, green acres rolling away from his feet. As the words sank in, their meaning crystalized. It was so obvious. *Of course! God gave us this land to start a farm here. The food will feed the Karen. But there's far more land here than they will need. The surplus can be sold to offset expenses, even pay our mortgage!*

It began to rain. Michael hurried back up the knoll. His first step would need to be a phone call to Michael Williams, now his senior warden and trusted advisor. But by the time he reached the church door, a new thought asserted itself. *He's going to think I'm crazy.*

Well, if he was crazy, Michael Williams would tell him, and then he could get back to working on his budget. After all, Michael Williams not only had decades of ministry experience, but much of it had been in America's farming heartland. He'd undoubtedly be quick to point out the flaws in such a plan.

But when Michael told Michael Williams about his walk and how God had told him to start a farm to feed people and help cover expenses, the senior warden's response was unexpected. "You need to call the bishop. Right now."

"Are you kidding?" Michael argued back. "I just spent two hours on the phone with him yesterday. We talked this thing round and round, looking for any other way forward besides selling, and we kept coming back to the same conclusion: we have no other options. I kind of thought you would tell me I'm crazy, but I know he will."

"No, you get him on the phone, and call me back after you've spoken to him," Michael Williams countered flatly, then hung up the telephone.

❊ ❊ ❊

For his part, Michael Williams could indeed see countless pitfalls ahead. But he also had absolutely no doubt this young priest who was his vicar had indeed heard the voice of God. Sometimes it took a crisis to get people to listen to God. And a crisis was certainly what faced All Saints right now. That this epiphany had come on Pentecost, which celebrated the descent of God's Holy Spirit on his church, seemed even more appropriate. It was as though the Spirit of God had descended over All Saints to say bluntly, "Hey there, I've got work for you to do."

❊ ❊ ❊

With grave misgivings, Michael Spurlock called the diocese and asked to speak with Bishop Bauerschmidt. To his surprise, the bishop was quick to take his call. Michael told the bishop what he had told Michael Williams. Bishop Bauerschmidt heard him out without interrupting. Then Michael waited for the bishop's response. The decision to sell or keep All Saints was not, after all, in Michael's hands nor even those of the All Saints congregation. It wasn't even the bishop's decision alone, but that of the same diocesan council that had given them permission to sell the church property. If Michael had misheard God's message, their response would make it clear.

But once again, the bishop's reply was hardly what Michael expected. "Michael, isn't it just like God to show up at the eleventh hour!"

The words brought tears to Michael's eyes. The bishop continued, "I've never been able to muster much enthusiasm for selling All Saints, but I have great enthusiasm for this idea."

By the end of their discussion, Bishop Bauerschmidt had outlined the necessary steps for placing a hold on any decision to accept the offer on the property, as well as for Michael and his congregation to present this plan to the Bishop and Council, as the diocesan leadership council was termed. Their next meeting was a week from Saturday. Michael would also need to address his own congregation to gauge their support. With all the unexpected reactions he'd experienced over these past two hours, Michael was no longer worried his congregation would be much of a hurdle at all.

But there was another phone call he needed to make first, and that was to Ye Win. "You asked if the Karen could plant gardens to feed their families. How would they feel about starting a farm?" Once again, Michael explained his plan.

Ye Win's response was positive, but cautious. "Yes, this is good."

"But will your community get behind it?" Michael pressured. "It will be a lot of hard work. And I know nothing about farming. We would need their expertise."

"I will ask them."

By the time Ye Win called back, Michael was already working up his proposal for the diocesan council. As with his original pitch to sell the property, he prepared graphs, spelled out costs and profit margins. Perhaps a little optimistic for someone with no real experience, but hopefully his own enthusiasm would be contagious.

"Once I explained it to them, they agreed they will do this," Ye Win communicated. Michael wasn't surprised. Even in these few weeks, it had become clear that Ye Win was the *de facto* leader of Smyrna's Karen community. Where he went, the others would follow. And maybe not only the Karen.

※ ※ ※

It was long after Aimee had expected him home for dinner when Michael walked through the front door. She'd known just how hard Michael would find this meeting with the buyers, so she'd been increasingly concerned as the hours passed. But instead of depressed, her husband looked exhilarated as he entered the house.

"I think I've got good news!" he announced. "We don't have to sell the church!"

Aimee stared at him, stunned. "How is that possible?"

"God told me to start a farm."

Aimee knew her husband well, and he didn't appear to be joking. She asked cautiously, "How? You know nothing about farming."

"I have no idea. I just know God told us to do it."

Michael's smile was more carefree and joyous than Aimee had seen since the decision had been made to sell All Saints. She broke off her first instinct to protest as she remembered other times she'd seen that same assurance in his eyes, that same joy in his smile. When he'd told her God was calling him to seminary. When he'd accepted the appointment to Nashotah House and then to All Saints. She'd never yet regretted following her husband as he followed God. She would not start today.

Aimee met her husband's smile with a radiant smile of her own. "Then let's do it."

❋ ❋ ❋

Years later, when All Saints had become a national news story and in time a movie script, Michael was asked how he'd been so sure what he'd heard was God speaking and not just some idea birthed in his own mind from his own desires.

"Because I know me," Michael answered, "and that wasn't me! Each one of us knows the sound of his own voice constantly sounding in his or her own head. I've lived in my head all my life, and I know its tone and timbre. What I heard was larger than myself and came from outside myself. This voice was not my voice. It was not me. It was his voice. It's just that simple.

"But that's not even the remarkable thing to me. God has a long record of speaking to mankind. What's remarkable was that this broken, willful pilgrim, who had once told God to butt out, was actually listening and willing to do what he said. Now, that's a miracle!"

19

Of course there was far more to it, and Michael would quickly discover that the greatest challenges had not yet even surfaced. Sunday came, and during the usual announcement segment, Michael addressed the congregation. "We need to talk a moment." Ye Win translated his words to the Karen membership. "I have a simple question for you. I want to ask you what you might be willing to do so that we don't have to sell the church and property."

Michael waited for a response. Dan Erickson, a kindly and enthusiastic parishioner, spoke up immediately. "We'd do anything!"

There were nods and murmurs of agreement. Michael rubbed his hands together. "Then listen to this."

Michael shared once more the story of his walk around the property, his experience with God, his idea for the farm, as well as the positive reactions from Michael Williams, Bishop Bauerschmidt, and Ye Win. He explained that he'd been invited to present this plan to the Bishop and Council the following Saturday, but he did not feel he could ask for permission to halt the sale and embark on this project without the parish's consultation, consent, and enthusiasm.

Stunned silence erupted into spontaneous applause. Tears began to flow. Smiles broke out on faces. Neighbor turned to neighbor and began excited conversations. Michael called them back to order. "Is that a yes?"

It turned out to be more than a yes. It was a *unanimous* yes!

To Michael, that moment would mark the turning point for All Saints. The church had survived loss and grief, upheaval and change. Now it was time to really begin getting All Saints back to health and life and growth.

When Michael headed into Nashville the next Saturday for the Bishop and Council meeting, he was accompanied by Michael Williams, Ye Win, and Ye Win's father, John Kunoo. All Saints was hardly the only item on the council's agenda. Just ahead of them was another parish asking for a $25,000 loan to add a modest Sunday school room onto their church. To Michael's mind, the council's questioning was severe and unsympathetic. How did the church plan to repay the loan? Was such an expansion absolutely necessary? What was the additional space to be used for? Was this a wise use of diocesan funds? What benefits did the parish expect from the addition?

Wow, if it's this hard for a self-supporting parish without a large mortgage to get a loan of $25,000, we're doomed! Michael groaned inwardly. *Why would they ever stop a property sale on a mission encumbered to the tune of $850,000?*

By the time the other church group had finished, Michael was dreading his own presentation. But he gathered himself up and began to speak. The expressions on the rest of his team's faces offered silent support as he laid out their history and vision, from the fallout of All Saints' split to the arrival of the Karen, the message he'd heard from God, and their long-term plans and budget for the farm.

Once he'd finished, Michael Williams and Ye Win were each given an opportunity to speak. In his strongly accented English, Ye Win spoke simply about his people. Their escape from oppression and genocide. Their love of Jesus. The home they had found at All Saints. Their skills as farmers and joy at the possibility of working this land.

When all three finished, Michael steeled himself for the upcoming interrogation. But it did not come, at least not yet. In front of

Michael, the council members were seated down both sides of a long table. Among them, Bishop Bauerschmidt's expression had been serene throughout the presentation, and Michael knew he had the bishop's support. But it was the faces of the other council members that showed a complete transformation. More than one had tears in their eyes. The atmosphere in the room was no longer that of brisk, no-nonsense business.

Then one of the council members spoke. "This is one of the most inspiring stories I've ever heard."

His words were echoed by others around the table. With very little further discussion, the Bishop and Council rescinded the decision to sell the All Saints property.

The Bible says that God turns the hearts of kings to his purposes (Proverbs 21:1), Michael reminded himself. *If this is from God, he can turn the hearts of council members too!*

Of course, there were still hard questions to answer. Zoning ordinances. Permits. Land use regulations. Budgets. Finance. Expected expenses and expected yields. On and on, the questions came. The small party from All Saints had few answers, but mercifully, the council did not require answers to make the necessary decision. They simply charged the All Saints team to get to work and report back in one month's time.

Other conditions included returning to next month's council meeting with a five-year business plan, answers to the questions that needed resolving, and a commitment from All Saints that they would not make any requests for additional funds to support the farming project.

"You may not ask us for any money," the council warned.

"We won't," Michael promised. But already he was beginning to wonder just where they were to find start-up costs. Even if the All Saints congregation supplied grunt labor, there were costs of seed, tools, irrigation equipment. A tractor would be necessary to plow up the Bermuda grass lawns that currently held softball diamonds. And information was needed as well. The Karen might be farmers, but growing conditions and marketable crops differed considerably from Myanmar, where seasons varied only from rainy to dry, to Tennessee's four-season climate.

But what All Saints most needed, they'd now been granted: the time and freedom to pursue God's vision.

The next week had already been scheduled months earlier for the Spurlocks' annual vacation. With little that could be done until the follow-up meeting with the diocesan council, the family left as planned to visit one of Aimee's brothers, Peter, who worked in the government in Washington, DC. Michael no longer doubted that God had spoken to him. But he found himself still bracing for someone to tell him just how naïve he was being. Wouldn't someone stop him before all this got too far along? Michael Williams. Bishop Bauerschmidt. Ye Win. The parish. The diocesan council. He'd expected any and all of them to put on the brakes. But they hadn't.

Peter and his wife, Karen, had arranged a dinner party for their visit. Among the guests was an official from the US Department of Agriculture. *Okay, so back in our small pond of Smyrna, they think I'm not crazy. Let me test the idea on a real expert in the field.* During dinner, Michael told his story. But instead of shooting it down, the Department of Agriculture official was immediately enthusiastic.

"That is one of the greatest project ideas anyone's ever pitched to me," he told Michael.

Aimee's brother was in agreement. If Michael didn't need their confirmation, he certainly appreciated their encouragement. He was beginning to feel he might not be so crazy after all.

While the Spurlocks were in DC, Michael Williams was back in Tennessee, setting up a meeting with the Rutherford County Soil Conservation Agency for when Father Michael returned. Once again, they would be pitching their plan to professionals. And not necessarily churchgoing professionals who might be open to a story of God speaking from heaven!

But by now, Michael wasn't even surprised when the board expressed enthusiasm and interest rather than pessimism. The meeting had been set up simply to ask for information and guidance. But the board eagerly informed the two Michaels of a brand-new project of their own. CROP, an acronym for Conservation Resources Outreach Program, had been inaugurated less than three months earlier, in March 2008, for the express purpose of offering technical and financial assistance in the fields of conservation and agriculture. So far, CROP had one charter member. Would All Saints be interested in becoming the second?

Michaels Spurlock and Williams walked out of the meeting with a sign identifying All Saints as a CROP project, as well as a $500 check. They'd also been assigned an advisor who would come out to the church to do soil testing and give counsel on which crops would grow best in their fields. If that wasn't enough, one of the board members approached after the meeting. Bruce Gentry owned one of Rutherford County's largest dairies.

"Did you know that All Saints was built on land I sold to the church ten years ago?" Bruce asked. "I used to farm that land, and I am so excited that you are returning it to the use for which God created it. In fact, I'd like to come out and plow it for you. Would next Monday work for you?"

Would it? Michael was beginning to think all he really needed to do was step out of God's way and let God work his plan!

20

One issue still did need to be dealt with before Bruce Gentry could plow up the fields. Michael called the parks and recreation department to request the removal of their softball backstops. For the first time, he encountered the resistance he'd anticipated throughout.

"We can't take them down now!" Michael was told. "We have those fields scheduled for use till the end of the year. You'll just have to wait until we can make other arrangements."

"No, I need them off by this weekend," Michael countered firmly.

"Hey, now look here! We've put a lot of investment into that property. You can't expect us to just pull up stakes and walk away. Besides, that's a big piece of land. You've hardly got the people or equipment to farm it all!"

"You also got a lot of free use of our land. And now we need it for our own use. But I'll tell you what I'll do," Michael conceded. "We're only going to plow half to start with. If you can get your backstops off that half by this weekend, you can use the other half till the end of the year. But be aware, we'll be expanding, so you'll need to move sooner or later."

By Friday, a city crew had arrived to pull up all the backstops. That weekend Michael walked down the knoll with Michael Williams to lay out the design for their farm. They chose to divide the acreage into four square plots, with pathways in between to create a cruciform shape. In the center would be a circular area where workers could come together to pray and worship, so that from an aerial view the design would be that of a simple cross. Maybe someday they could even erect a small chapel in the middle of these fields.

Monday morning, Bruce Gentry called. "Are those backstops off? We're ready to come out there and plow your fields."

By the end of the day, four acres were plowed and ready for seeding. Early that next Saturday morning, forty-five All Saints members, Karen and Anglo, young and old, gathered at the base of the church knoll. The $500 from CROP had been spent on hoes, rakes, shovels, and seeds. The crops they'd planned out with their agricultural advisor included green beans, lettuce, radishes, yellow squash, and cucumbers. The Karen contributed sour leaf, a staple in Southeast Asian cooking, its lemony-tart flowers, buds, and leaves used for pickling, curries, and other spicy dishes. Besides home use, this was a crop for which there was great commercial demand in Asian restaurants and stores.

This first planting had been designated for salad vegetables—lettuce, radishes, cucumbers. Each volunteer was given a task. Those Karen with farming experience took the lead hoeing furrows, placing each seed in place, raking over the freshly planted ground. Merry Adams in her power chair, Aimee, and other women with small children manned tables laden with snacks and drinks. The children formed a bucket chain with one-gallon watering cans to bring water up from the creek to empty into an old horse-watering trough that Michael's predecessor had used for outdoor baptisms, the Spurlocks' young son, Atticus, taking his turn with the others. Another brigade of adults carried the water to drench each freshly planted row.

That was when the murmuring started. This was now full summer in lowland Tennessee, the sky a cloudless blue overhead, which made temperatures soar as the day went on. The bank was a good ten to fifteen feet above the creek. Steps had been cut into the dirt to ease the trek up and down. But spilled water soon turned the climb into a slippery scramble. Water supply reaching the trough soon fell well behind need in the field.

By midday, an acre and a half of tilled ground had been planted. One small plot was chosen to plant all the sour leaf seeds. Once they germinated, each seedling would be transplanted into a larger field. Remaining acreage would be seeded the following week. But already the question was how a volunteer force could possibly keep up with watering so many furrows. However willing, the children were already worn out. And the adults weren't far behind.

The Anglo volunteers were the loudest with their complaints. "All this seed is just going to burn up in the ground. And we can't keep coming out here to water every day. Especially in this heat! We had no idea it would be this much work. How are we supposed to do this? It's just too much for us to handle!"

By the time the last bucket of water had been poured out and dirt-covered volunteers were wearily making their way back up the knoll to the church, Michael's earlier excitement had given way to dismay. The dissenters were right that there was no way their small group could adequately water all those acres by hand. Not in this heat. Something Michael would have foreseen, had he the smallest experience as a farmer.

God, you've brought us this far, he prayed. *Show us what to do next!*

That night the skies opened. No torrential downpour, but a deep, steady, gentle, soaking rain. Enough rain that the sprouting seedlings under their blanket of moisture-saturated earth would not need to.be watered for at least another week.

The next morning as the congregation gathered for worship, Michael opened *The Book of Common Prayer* to begin the service. In the Anglican tradition, the readings for each Sunday are predetermined by a fixed calendar. This week's readings began with the day's psalm:

You visit the earth and water it abundantly; you make it very plenteous; the river of God is full of water. You prepare the grain, for so you provide for the earth. You drench the furrows and smooth out the ridges; with heavy rain you soften the ground and bless its increase.

Psalm 65:9–11, *The Book of Common Prayer*, 1979

The stunning relevance of the day's psalm to their own situation could not be missed, and from the front of the church, Michael could see immediate realization and tears across his congregation. A reading from one of the New Testament epistles was then followed by this Sunday's gospel reading, which was one of Jesus' agricultural parables: "A sower went out to sow his seed."

"Hey, that's us!" rippled across the sanctuary. "That's just what we were doing yesterday!"

By now people were weeping. Yesterday they'd demanded to know how they were to accomplish this difficult task. Not in anger or rebellion, but with honest concern and bewilderment. Who could doubt now that God had given his answer? And not just to Michael, the vicar of this church, but to each member of the All Saints congregation. These verses from God's Word were as miraculous a provision as last night's rain.

21

That next weekend, another acre and a half had been planted in green beans and cucumbers, leaving the final acre for transplanting the sour leaf. Michael was still stunned at just how quickly it had all come together. When they'd first met with the Rutherford County Soil Conservation Agency, Bruce Gentry himself had warned them it could take years to start a farm. What a contrast to their own time line!

They'd received authorization from the bishop's council on a Saturday and met with the soil conservation agency that next Tuesday. Bruce Gentry had plowed their fields the following Monday. The first seed had been in the ground that next Saturday, the rest on the following Saturday. Three weeks total from the bishop's council to final planting. In fact, from the day Michael had taken that walk around the All Saints property and heard from God to the day they finished sowing three acres of seed in the ground had been just five weeks!

But the water issue still needed a long-term solution. The rains had not returned, and as the seedlings sprouted, they needed daily watering. Weeds were also springing up to choke out the fledgling crops. A pump would get water up the bank from the creek. A tiller would deal with the weeds. But Michael was conscious of his promise to the diocesan council to ask for no additional funds. Putting All Saints into further debt was even less acceptable.

A little money remained from the CROP check and some

other donations, about $800 in total. Michael talked over the problem with Michael Williams. "We've got funds to do one of two things. Either fix our watering problem or our weeding problem."

The two men decided to watch the weather for a sign. If it rained, they'd buy a tiller for $500 and start weeding. If it didn't rain, they'd have to buy a water pump for $800 to irrigate out of the creek. Both needs were becoming critical. But when the rains held off, it became clear the pump for watering was most urgent. They spent the last dime of savings to buy a pump and some hoses. These had just been installed when Michael saw a car pull up to the church. Its driver was a semi-retired priest, Father Tim, who'd been visiting in the area.

After greeting Michael, he went on, "I was just passing through on my way back to Nashville. I figured I'd stop just to say hello and see how you were doing down here."

"Come on out back, and I'll show you what we've been up to," Michael responded.

Michael guided his visitor around the fields, pointing out the various crops and giving some background on the Karen. The conversation was general, and Michael hadn't even mentioned any needs. But the very next day, a check for $500 arrived in the mail. It was from Father Tim. It was also the exact amount needed to purchase the tiller.

For Michael, it was a wake-up call. His thoughts flew back to seminary days, when God had also provided so unexpectedly. *Okay, God, you'd think I'd already learned this lesson. You are going to supply when we need it and not before, because you want us to travel light and live by faith.*

God's provision was not just financial. He had also sent people exactly when needed. Father Tim. Paul Adams to teach ESL. Michael Williams and Father Bu Christ, whose flexible schedules permitted them to pitch in during daytime hours. Ye Win drove in vanloads of Karen volunteers after their own hard day's work to put in some time weeding. Others like Merry Adams, who couldn't work the fields, pitched in with donations, administrative duties, and prayer.

Still, on a daily basis it was often just Michael making sure the growing seedlings were kept watered. And though the pump had solved the water problem, getting the water from the pump to the fields entailed basically running a firehose more than two hundred yards to each individual furrow. And doing so without crushing any neighboring plants. What they really needed was some kind of delivery system directly to the plants from a water tank. A small grant from an Episcopal mission trust made possible the purchase of a well-used 1958 tractor. But a water tank would be several thousand dollars more. Far out of reach for this summer's budget at least.

In early August, the All Saints congregation celebrated the harvesting of the first radishes. Michael and Father Bu Christ personally delivered four bushels to various Karen families. But Michael was finding himself increasingly exhausted, not just physically, but emotionally and spiritually. It seemed that his entire waking life had become consumed by this farm project.

Nor could Michael neglect other parish duties. He'd also begun helping Ye Win with the transportation needs of the Karen. The most distressing consequence was how little time was left to devote to his wife and his own growing family. And when they were together, Michael and Aimee's conversations always seemed to revert to what the next looming need was at church or the farm.

Mondays were technically Michael's day off, though that had meant little since starting the farm. But one Monday not long after that first radish delivery, Michael and Aimee made arrangements to drive up to a nearby state park and go for a hike. Fiery Gizzard Trail in South Cumberland State Park was an hour's drive from their home. As they parked the car, Michael said firmly, "Okay, no talking about church or the farm. And no getting social with strangers either. I don't want to see or talk to anyone but you."

As Michael had hoped, Monday morning was not a busy time for the park. Just one other family was headed for the trailhead, a young couple with a baby in a backpack carrier. Michael pulled Aimee back. "Let's wait to see which direction they go. Then we'll go in the other."

The plan worked, but an hour of hiking later, Michael spotted the young family advancing straight toward them on the trail up ahead. Of course! Since the trail formed a loop leading back to the entrance, it should have occurred to him that their path would run them right into the other family somewhere on the loop. Aimee was already smiling and looking alarmingly friendly.

Michael shot her a warning glance. "I don't want to engage here! Just say hello, nod politely, and move on."

As they reached the other couple, Michael nodded and smiled, preparing to pass on. But Aimee was already exclaiming, "Oh, what a cute baby! Is it a boy or a girl?"

Within seconds, the two women were deep in conversation. Michael stood there, exchanging awkward glances with the baby's father, mentally urging Aimee to wrap things up. As the minutes dragged on, the man asked Michael if he knew of a nearby camping site.

Michael told him he thought there was one. The man went on to explain that he used to camp in the park when he attended a nearby Episcopal high school. Michael had been to seminary with a fellow Tennessean he knew attended the same high school, so he asked the man if he knew Peter Floyd.

"Actually, yes, I went to high school with him," the man replied. "It's a small world! We're back visiting now from Missouri. My family has a farm there."

"Really? Our church just started a farm."

Michael had forgotten his vow not to talk farming. The two women were still going strong. So Michael began to share his church's story. The other man turned out to be Jason Bean, whose family owned one of Missouri's largest farming cooperatives, Bean Farms, with about 14,000 acres of soybean, rice, and corn. Michael felt a little foolish for bringing up All Saints' meager twenty-two acres. But Jason looked genuinely interested.

"It sounds like a great project," he commented when Michael was finished. "You know, as my farm has grown, we've got a lot of equipment we've outgrown. If there's anything you need, just let me know, and I'd be glad to let you have it."

"Well," Michael answered, "I do know one thing we could use. You wouldn't happen to have a thousand-gallon water tank mounted on a trailer with a pump attached, do you?"

"As a matter of fact, I do have a thousand-gallon water tank," Jason responded. "And it's on a trailer and has a pump mounted to it. You can arrange to haul it back from Missouri."

The two men exchanged contact information. Then the two families said their good-byes and went their separate ways. Michael was as stunned as he was exhilarated. He had come out to this wilderness to get as far away as possible from his vocation, his church, the farm, and, in truth, God's claim on his life, even if just for a few hours. And yet God had followed him out here, reminding Michael that there was no place where God was not present and sovereign.

It was a thought that was at once harrowing and exciting to Michael. He'd never thought of himself as some kind of Moses. But he could now imagine what it must have felt like to be led by God into the wilderness and asked to strike a barren dry rock so that water might gush out to quench the thirst of millions.

When Michael explained to Aimee what had happened with Jason, Aimee was quick to respond, "And you didn't want me to talk with them!" She couldn't help but smile. And neither could Michael. For once, he could actually enjoy an "I told you so."

As they continued on down the trail, Michael was now almost eager to meet someone else on the path. Sure enough, he soon spotted a family of hikers approaching.

"Hello! How are you all doing today?" Michael greeted them with a broad smile. "What a beautiful day this is!" He really felt like proclaiming, "Hello. I'm Father Michael Spurlock. Do you have something God has told you to give me?"

Not since that moment in May when God had spoken to him

about starting the farm had Michael sensed so strongly God's presence, reminding him that this was God's plan, not Michael's. God's farm, not Michael's.

And that became the name of All Saints' farming project: Kurios Farms. The Greek word for "lord," *kurios* was a common word for God in the original language of the New Testament. A reminder to Michael, his parish, and the world that this was God's farm and God was in charge of it.

22

Retrieving the water tank proved an adventure of its own.
Or more like a comedy of errors.

In anticipation of hauling home a trailer, Michael had borrowed his grandfather's pickup truck. The Bean farm in Holcomb, near the Missouri-Arkansas border, was a four-hour drive from All Saints in good traffic. So an early start should mean a return well before dark. Father Bu Christ had volunteered to accompany Michael. The two men got the planned early start, arriving at the Bean farm well before midday.

That was when the first snag made itself known. The trailer was bigger than Michael had anticipated and had no taillights of its own. To pull it down the freeway attached to the pickup required taillights. No problem. They should be able to pick up lights at the closest auto parts store, attach them to the trailer's rear, plug them into a circuit connection under the pickup bed, and get on their way again with minimal delay.

Father Bu Christ helped Michael hook the trailer to the pickup. After thanking Jason, they headed into town. A light rain had turned into a full downpour by the time Michael had purchased the lights. He crawled under the truck, getting soaking wet in the process, only to discover that the plug-in connector for the lights did not match that of the pickup.

Michael returned to the store to make an exchange. There he was informed that the store didn't have the correct attachment in stock. In the driving rain, they drove on next to Walmart, then Kmart, neither of which had the necessary connector. It was two hours later before they finally found an auto parts store that carried it.

By the time the lights were hooked up and working it was mid-afternoon, and both Michael and Father Bu Christ were thoroughly drenched. Still, the days were long this time of year, and even taking into account the inclement weather, they should make it back to All Saints before dark. And they would have if, in the continuing deluge, Michael hadn't mistaken the turn onto the Interstate. They'd driven an hour northeast toward Kentucky instead of southeast toward Smyrna before Michael realized his error.

Getting off the Interstate, Michael headed cross-country, orienting his direction by putting the setting sun at their back. By now he was thoroughly lost, and he had neither a map nor GPS to reorient himself. All he could do was look for signs that might lead them to the correct Interstate heading south.

The rain continued. So did the wind. The trailer tires were bald, and the wind's updraft kept catching at the trailer, sending it shimmying back and forth across the road. By the time Michael finally spotted a sign that pointed him toward the correct Interstate, he was not so confident they'd survive the trip. The open freeway proved even more blustery than the side roads, and Michael had to slow to a crawl to keep the trailer from jackknifing.

In all this, Father Bu Christ had hardly spoken a word. Michael's invitation for Father Bu Christ to accompany him had been good-intentioned. An opportunity for the two priests who ministered to All Saints' two language groups to spend some quality time together. Michael might even learn a bit more about his brother in Christ in the process.

But till now, Ye Win had typically been around to help interpret, so Michael hadn't taken into account Father Bu Christ's minimal English skills. Barring the occasional nod, smile, or hand gestures, they'd spent the drive to Missouri in silence. This return trip was little different. Was Father Bu Christ finding Michael's driving as nerve-wracking as Michael did? If so, his stoic expression did not betray it.

It was well after dark and still raining hard when they finally reached All Saints around eleven p.m. But at least they were still in one piece, and the rain meant no watering tomorrow. The two men unhitched the trailer. Then Michael dropped off Father Bu Christ and headed home.

Never send two priests to do the work of one farmer! Michael told himself humorously as he crawled exhausted into bed beside Aimee. But at least he and Father Bu Christ had done it, and they'd done it together. Sometimes mutual survival did more to forge a bond than a dictionary of words!

❋ ❋ ❋

In the end, it was Paul Adams who would first learn Father Bu Christ's full story, and he learned it from an unexpected source. The evening ESL program had started. On the first night, seven families showed up. Paul's original concept had been to set up a regular classroom setting with books and homework. But the group ranged from preschool through elderly, illiterate through college graduates, and it quickly became clear that no one-size-fits-all format would work. Instead, Paul decided to focus on Living in America 101. He would discuss with Ye Win what the group most needed, then focus on that topic—Paul explaining, Ye Win translating.

One such topic was bank cards. The Karen had discovered ATMs, but their practice was to withdraw the minimum they needed to spend. They felt dismayed and cheated when fees began to accrue, since a $20 withdrawal resulted in the same fee as $1,000. Many could not read in Karen, much less English.

Paul took his own ATM card to the class. He pointed out the bank logo on the front. "See this picture? You can take out just $20 if you like. But only if the picture on your card matches the picture on the ATM."

Problem solved! For another class, the Karen had asked for a rundown on snakes. The Karen knew cobras and pythons, but not which snakes to avoid in the Tennessee countryside. So Paul researched and taught a class on how to tell the difference between venomous pit vipers and equally scary-looking but harmless king and rat snakes. A number of the Karen had found work at the Tyson poultry plant and needed to know terminology, so another evening was devoted to learning the names of each chicken part.

Other topics included how to apply for a job and what response was expected on forms to such acronyms as DOB and SSN. Simply learning how to fill out a form was invaluable, since the Karen had already been plagued by scam artists charging them huge sums to fill out necessary paper work. Paul also taught how the American constitution and government worked. To see eyes light up as his audience grasped just who "we, the people" were and that they too could aspire to be citizens was a rewarding moment.

Paul made arrangements as well for local police to stop in and meet the Karen. In Myanmar and Thailand, the Karen had learned to fear the police, well-known for their corruption and brutality. That there was any point in calling the police when trouble broke out was in itself a new concept.

One particular incident at the Chalet Apartments encapsulated the problem. A particularly nasty gang of local drug dealers had decided that these much slighter, shorter, brown-skinned people from across the ocean, who couldn't even speak decent English, were the perfect shakedown targets. They hadn't taken into consideration the fact that a number of these particular refugees were not just traumatized refugees but experienced guerrilla fighters. By the time the police, no strangers to the Chalet Apartments, arrived on the scene, no guns were in sight, but the hardened drug dealers who'd been terrorizing the complex were inexplicably on the run.

And indeed, not all Karen were angels nor even law-abiding churchgoers like the All Saints congregation. There were Karen youth suffering from PTSD, struggling with drug and alcohol addiction, and getting into trouble, including fights at school. With his own military background, Paul Adams made it a priority to foster good relations and trust between the Karen and local law enforcement.

How successful he'd been became evident one day when he spotted a police car that had pulled over a vanload of Karen. Not unusual, unfortunately. The Karen weren't used to wasting space on just one person per seat belt or obeying other traffic laws they considered suggestions more than ultimatums, so what a traffic ticket meant had been another teaching topic. Recognizing some of the Karen, Paul pulled over to see if there was any help he could offer. But as he did so, he spotted the police officer crawling out from under the vehicle—where he'd been helping the Karen change a flat tire.

Though he was enjoying this new ESL experience, Paul had made one thing clear from the beginning: he didn't work with kids. The school-age Karen had learned some English in the refugee camps but struggled with American slang and culture. Paul roped in a few Anglo teenagers to answer their questions and tutor them in their homework.

That was where Paul came into contact with Father Bu Christ's oldest son. Fifteen years old when their family arrived in Smyrna, Ba Soh Wah was struggling with his first year of American high school. But his English was improving so quickly he soon acquired a Tennessee drawl, and he began to be called upon as a translator when Ye Win wasn't available.

To all appearances, Ba Soh Wah seemed a typical teen, though perhaps more hardworking, studious, and respectful than his average American counterpart. But the bits of his past life he occasionally let slip dumbfounded Paul Adams.

One day he described his earliest memory to Paul, which had occurred at just three years of age. He'd awoken from a nap in their thatched-roof home when mortars from Burmese military cannon across the river that formed the Thai-Burmese border began raining down on the small refugee camp where they lived. His mother had slipped out to harvest food from a jungle garden plot that supplemented their diet. His father and older sister had headed over to the school Father Bu Christ administered.

Alone, Ba Soh Wah's first instinct was to hide from the explosions in a nearby water barrel. But he'd remembered his parents' instructions for such an event and scrambled instead to the safety of a nearby bunker, where his parents eventually retrieved him. And God had indeed saved him as well as the rest of his family.

Paul noted that same matter-of-fact faith from other children whose families had been part of Father Bu Christ's congregation in the camp. When they were asked what they remembered of their old lives, Paul had expected horrific stories and trauma.

Instead, they commented thoughtfully, "Well, I remember all the mud and rain walking to school and church. There weren't any paved roads. I remember the bamboo and thatched roofs and how green it all was."

When asked to amplify, their most common response was to shrug. "It was, well, different than here! The food was different. More spicy."

What impacted Paul Adams most was the lack of hate and bitterness directed toward their Burmese oppressors who'd burned these people out from home and country. Sure, the Bible talked about loving your enemies. But these people were actual living proof that it could be done.

It all led back to Father Bu Christ himself, whose story Paul was learning in bits and pieces from Ba Soh Wah or in conversations with Father Bu Christ translated by his son. If Ye Win was the leader of this refugee community, Father Bu Christ was most evidently its spiritual shepherd. So who was this man? Could the faith and forgiveness he professed—and which Paul himself had long dismissed as human hypocrisy—actually be genuine?

23

In truth, being anyone's spiritual shepherd was the last career choice a young Thomas Bu Christ had ever had in mind. Like Ye Win, Bu Christ's Christian heritage stretched back to the early twentieth century, when British Anglican missionaries had brought the gospel to his great-grandparents. Bu Christ himself was named after the disciple who had first brought the gospel to Asia after the resurrection of Jesus Christ.

When Thomas was born in 1951, sixth of eight siblings, the British were long gone. The year he turned fifteen, Burma's military junta expelled all remaining expatriate missionaries and began its campaign of persecution against Christians. But Bu Christ's family remained faithful. His younger brother had decided to become an Anglican priest, as had one uncle and a cousin. Other family members were deacons, church lay leaders, traveling evangelists.

Thomas had no intention of following that family heritage. Once he'd exhausted the education available in his mountain village, his parents encouraged him to study for Christian ministry at St. Peter's Bible School in Taungoo, a city in the north of Karen territory. An institution of Christian higher education for the Karen since 1893, St. Peter's had been razed to the ground by the Japanese during World War II, then relocated to several different villages during the civil war that followed. After another long closure, it had just reopened back in Taungoo.

Thomas was not interested. Determined to go his own way, he

left home, eventually finding work in a mine. He'd been there just a year when word came that the Burmese military had attacked his home territory, burning numerous villages. Furious, he headed home, determined to enlist in the Karen rebel army. His father forbade him to enlist, so instead he joined as a camp follower, helping carry supplies or setting land mines. Eventually, he began farming a plot of land. But his parents were still urging Thomas to leave the conflict zone and attend St. Peter's.

"You know, the Bible says that if you honor your parents, your life will be long in the land" (Exodus 20:12), his local rector encouraged him. Theology was not a topic that interested Thomas. But neither was he satisfied with his life's current dead-end direction. At age twenty-two, he packed up his meager possessions and headed to St. Peter's.

What Thomas found was a shell of the original St. Peter's. A few wood buildings had been erected. There were only twenty-five students his first year and two teachers, one of them his uncle. Since the expatriate staff had all left the country, education was now in Karen with no English, a factor that would shape Father Bu Christ's future. The dormitory was a simple bamboo hall lined with mats and mosquito nets. With jungle pressing in on all sides, the students were required to spend mornings studying and afternoons cutting back the brush and farming the cleared land. Despite their hard work, food was scant—rarely more than rice with fish paste, along with peppers and other vegetables they managed to grow.

Even so, by the end of the first year, Thomas no longer yearned to escape. It was in studying the apostle Paul that he found his own life calling. This first missionary had been a man of faith. A leader. A man who sacrificed for others. And his example was one that Thomas now yearned to emulate. He graduated from St. Peter's in 1976, then went on to attend Holy Cross Theological College in Rangoon. He'd committed his life to take the gospel of Jesus Christ, if not like the apostle Paul to the ends of the known world, at least to the ends of Burmese territory.

Over the following decade, Thomas became an itinerant Bible

teacher, starting churches and leading worship services in Karen villages where the gospel had not yet reached. The parish to which he'd been assigned encompassed sixteen scattered villages, which necessitated countless hours climbing up and down mountain trails. He received no salary or missionary support, so, like the villagers to whom he ministered, Thomas farmed a small plot of land, growing bamboo, rice, durian fruit, coffee, papaya, mango, and betel nut.

But trouble followed Thomas wherever he went. The Burmese military dominated the countryside, raiding villages, seizing crops and animals, driving refugees into the cities or across the border into refugee camps. Because Thomas was Karen, the Burmese assumed he must be spying for the Karen revolutionary army. Conversely, because he was not fighting with the Karen, Karen nationalists accused him of spying for the Burmese.

On one of his preaching circuits, Thomas was seized by a Burmese army unit. Someone in the unit was clearly sympathetic to Christian clergy, Karen or otherwise, as Thomas was eventually released. But not before the army unit forced him to serve as their translator while they raided surrounding villages, since Thomas was fluent in Burmese as well as Karen.

On another occasion, Thomas had planned a trip into the city to visit his family. He'd been given letters to deliver to other Karen in the city from their own family members, which he'd placed inside a book to carry. When he reached the city, he was stopped at a military checkpoint. A search turned up the letters. Insisting he was smuggling communications from the Karen revolutionary army, the checkpoint guards arrested Thomas and threw him into jail. There he remained until the local Anglican bishop intervened to bail him out.

Diocese leadership decided Thomas had risked his life in the countryside long enough. They transferred him back to the city, but Thomas was not happy. His desire remained to take the gospel to those who had never heard, not to live comfortably in a city that had plenty of churches and even Christian schools. Several of his friends from seminary were serving as missionaries on the Burmese-Thai border, traveling into remote mountain villages where no missionary had ever been. Thomas joined them. Over the following year, they saw many people come to Christ.

This was 1988, the height of the pro-democracy student uprising as well as the Burmese military's scorched-earth campaign against the Karen. Assault helicopters, tanks, and long-range cannon were taking their toll on the Karen rebel forces. Many of the villages where Thomas and his companions had preached the gospel were now charred rubble.

Thomas joined the flood of refugees crossing into Thailand. That was where he met Hae Htoo Pi, a war orphan who, like so many others, had been taken in as a child by the Karen revolutionary army. Raised and educated in a KNLA orphanage, she'd chosen the field of nursing to better serve the thousands of refugees driven out by the same brutal regime that had killed her parents. Hae Htoo Pi had become a Christian while at the orphanage and was attending a church in the refugee camp when mutual friends there introduced her to Thomas. They were married on May 24, 1990, along with three other couples. Like Hae Htoo Pi, the other brides were all nurses and war orphans raised as "daughters" by the Karen army, so the Karen high command took care of all wedding expenses.

The refugee camp became home for the couple. Their oldest daughter was born in 1991, their son Ba Soh Wah in 1993. Living in the camp placed no limits on Thomas's ministry as a missionary and evangelist. With many of the villagers Thomas had led to Christ now in the camp themselves—along with a growing population of young children—Thomas founded a Christian school as well as an orphanage, and Hae Htoo Pi worked as a nurse. While refugees were technically confined to camp, Thomas continued his missionary trips back across the border as well as into Karen villages on the Thai side.

24

With the Burmese military pushing ever deeper into Karen territory, the border camps were becoming dangerous. Neither the Karen nor the Thai had troops to mount a proper perimeter defense, and long-range mortars were routinely shelling the camps. Shortly after Ba Soh Wah's early memory of mortar shells and concrete bunkers, the border camps were evacuated to a much larger UN-sponsored camp, Mae La, deep enough into Thai territory to be out of reach of Burmese artillery. Another son and daughter were born to Thomas and Hae Htoo Pi there.

To Ba Soh Wah and his siblings, Mae La was the only home they'd known. And since they'd known no alternative, they saw few of its drawbacks. In fact, there were plenty of good memories to draw on. The camp's population was that of a sizeable city, growing over the next decade to fifty thousand residents. There were schools and numerous churches—not just Anglican, but Baptist, Methodist, Catholic, Seventh-Day Adventists—as well as places of worship for Hindu, Buddhist, and Muslim residents.

The UN refugee agency (UNHCR) provided a basic food allowance. If not lavish, it meant that no one went truly hungry, and the camp residents supplemented the rations of rice, oil, and fish paste by growing vegetables on any available garden plot. Even better, there were no soldiers shooting guns or lobbing mortars, at least within the barbed wire confines of the camp.

Church was the focus around which all daily life revolved. The Anglican church in the camp was large and also hosted a large Christian school, which Ba Soh Wah and his siblings attended. The rector in charge of the church and school when Thomas and his family arrived was elderly and soon appointed Thomas as his successor. Not long after, Thomas was ordained as a full priest. His own children quickly became accustomed to hearing other children and adults address him as Father Bu Christ.

The family now lived on the church compound. Sundays were spent in morning-till-evening worship services. There were also weeknight youth outreaches, prayer meetings, and Bible studies. Holidays like Easter and Christmas involved lavish celebrations with singing, drama, and dance. Under Father Bu Christ's leadership, attendance grew to over three hundred.

Ba Soh Wah didn't always appreciate having to sit through every church service while camp friends were out kicking a soccer ball through dusty streets, and he occasionally snuck out of church to join them. Still, his best memories involved accompanying his father on ministry rounds. Medical care was scarce in the camp, and he witnessed sick people healed as his father and other church leaders prayed over them. He also witnessed spiritual and emotional healings as his father shared Christ's love with grieving, hurting refugees.

Nor was the camp's barbed wire fence around the perimeter the boundary of Father Bu Christ's ministry. The camp's guards inside were Karen, the outside, Thai military. To leave the camp involved showing both ID and travel permits. But the Thai guards were not early risers. Before dawn, Father Bu Christ would lead a group, including Ba Soh Wah, through the gate. Hand-woven satchels held food for the trip, along with Christian literature and other supplies.

The team would hike into isolated Karen villages on both the Thai and Burmese sides of the border, preaching the gospel, praying for the sick, and offering basic medical aid to villagers with access to neither doctors nor medication. Ba Soh Wah's own faith grew as he saw God answer prayer again and again.

So as the years went by for the Bu Christ family, life was good. Life was steady. Life was even reasonably safe. But that became an increasing concern to Father Bu Christ. To his children, to his flock, the refugee camp had become not just home, but a normal and accepted lifestyle.

They'd now been in the camp for over fifteen years. Father Bu Christ's children had all been born in Thailand. Yet the Thai government refused to grant citizenship to Burmese refugees. Nor would the Burmese government welcome them back. However comfortable their current situation, the Bu Christ children would soon be adults without a country, unable to work or live outside the no-man's-land of the refugee camp, much less have opportunities for higher education than the school Father Bu Christ oversaw. If there was to be any chance of his children building a long-term new life, some alternative to a refugee camp must be found.

By 2007 the United Nations resettlement program was offering Karen and other Burmese refugees visas to a variety of countries. Reluctant though they were to leave behind church and school, Thomas and Hae Htoo Pi Bu Christ made the decision to apply. Father Bu Christ had relatives in Australia. But the waiting list for that country was long, while the United States had thrown its doors wide open to the Karen. And members of their congregation, the Kunoo family, had a son, Ye Win, already in the United States, who was willing to help other Karen settle there.

By September 2007, the Bu Christ family had passed their medicals, immigration interviews, and security check. They'd been assigned for resettlement in Louisville, Kentucky. But when they arrived there, the family was overwhelmed by the strangeness, the isolation from other Karen and anyone else they knew, the inability to communicate. Even finding food was bewildering since there were no proper open-air markets to purchase fresh vegetables, rice, and fish.

John and Daisy Kunoo, who had already arrived in the United States, had given Father Bu Christ their son's phone number. Locating a telephone, Father Bu Christ called the number. Ba Soh

Wah remembers Ye Win's father, John Kunoo, along with another friend, showing up at the small apartment they'd been assigned.

"Come stay with us. We'll help you get situated," John Kunoo assured them. "The Karen people in Smyrna need you. We have no church or anyone to teach God's Word."

With little to pack, the Bu Christ family left that same day. Only years later did Ba Soh Wah learn that new refugees were expected to stay where they'd been placed, at least until they'd learned to stand on their own feet and become somewhat assimilated. What their assigned sponsor thought when they showed up to find an empty apartment, Ba Soh Wah never learned.

The following months were the most difficult of his young life. Fifteen-year-old Ba Soh Wah had never been afraid sneaking past military checkpoints to share the gospel in high mountain villages. But his faith was stretched to the limit as he struggled to understand this strange new country, culture, language. At school, these Tennessee natives weren't always friendly to the black-haired, brown-skinned foreigners invading their personal space. And fifteen was old to be learning a new language while maintaining a passing grade in high-school-level studies.

That was when Ba Soh Wah met Paul Adams. And when he learned that this new country also had followers of Jesus Christ who could be as kind, loving, and sacrificial as the Christians he'd known back in the refugee camp. People who were no blood relation and who knew as little about the Karen as Ba Soh Wah knew of America, yet were willing to give time and finances to drive the Karen to church and the grocery store. Help Ba Soh Wah and his siblings with their homework. Fight bureaucracy on their behalf to obtain badly needed medical care for his father's injured back.

At All Saints the Bu Christ family once again had a church home, however different from the noisy, teeming wood-and-bamboo structure back at the camp. And they were once again part of a community, with some familiar faces that had been part of the Mae La congregation and some new friends, both Karen and Anglo.

"Here at All Saints is where my faith became real," Ba Soh Wah shares today. "Seeing so many strangers showing Christ's love and being willing to help us. My faith in God became my own and not just my parents'. I prayed and prayed to God for help. Prayed for him to help me learn English. And he answered my prayers and helped me learn more quickly than any of the others. I don't know where I would be today, or my family, if God had not brought us to Smyrna and to All Saints. Without our knowing or expecting, God is always planning for our lives ahead of time. We never expected back then we'd be where we are now as a family. And we don't know what is coming next. But God always knows our future, so we trust everything to him."

25

While Ba Soh Wah had found renewed faith through the example of Christ's love shown to the Karen by All Saints' Anglo congregation and others, Paul Adams was experiencing the reverse. The genuineness of these people's faith drew him. He'd spent his life complaining that the Christian life was too hard to live. But here were Father Bu Christ and others who at any time could have curried favor with their totalitarian regime by converting *from* Christianity, but instead risked their lives daily to live and share their faith, and whose response to injustice and the loss of homes, loved ones, country was to pray for their oppressors.

Paul soon found himself accompanying his wife, Merry, to worship services. He attended "house blessings," services of dedication held any time a Karen family moved into a home of their own. This was becoming more common as steady jobs made it possible for many Karen to leave the Chalet Apartments. Though he understood not a word, he attended some of the Karen home meetings, which Father Bu Christ led Sunday afternoons.

But if the rest of the congregation believed he was now a convert, Paul Adams knew otherwise. He'd called himself an agnostic rather than an atheist, as he'd never denied God's existence. It was hypocrisy he had an issue with, his own as much as that of others. And since he was only too well aware he'd hardly lived the exemplary Christian life he'd been taught growing up, he'd always believed it would be hypocritical to claim the Christian faith for himself.

One day when Paul was in Father Michael's office discussing the latest needs of the Karen, Michael broached the subject. "You say you aren't a believer, but you do believe in Jesus, don't you?"

"Yes," Paul admitted.

Father Michael pulled out a copy of the Nicene Creed, which Paul had repeated along with the rest of the All Saints congregation as part of the worship service every Sunday. "So let me just read this to you. Tell me if there is anything in here you *don't* believe."

He began intoning the beautiful acclamation of faith that Christians had recited in countless languages for more than fifteen hundred years. "We believe in one God, the Father, the Almighty, maker of heaven and earth, of all that is, seen and unseen."

Yes, he could agree with that, Paul admitted.

"We believe in one Lord, Jesus Christ, the only Son of God, eternally begotten of the Father. . . . For our sake he was crucified under Pontius Pilate; he suffered death and was buried. On the third day he rose again in accordance with the Scriptures."

If Paul had at times doubted the historicity of the Gospels, he could acknowledge now that he believed wholeheartedly in the biblical Jesus. One by one, Father Michael read off the remaining points.

"We believe in the Holy Spirit, the Lord, the giver of life. . . . We believe in one holy catholic and apostolic Church. We acknowledge one baptism for the forgiveness of sins. We look for the resurrection of the dead, and the life of the world to come."

By the end, Paul was stunned to realize there was indeed nothing he could not accept in the Nicene Creed. Father Michael didn't rub it in. He simply smiled. "So you're not really such an agnostic."

No he wasn't. That was the turning point for Paul Adams. The change in him was not overnight. And though Paul was well aware that his wife, Merry, and Father Michael were praying for him, both were astute enough not to nag him. But the more time he spent at All Saints and with the Karen, the more he realized that his own growing faith was far more than just an acceptance of biblical fact. *I love Jesus. I love God, and I want to follow him. And I love these people, the Karen, who have made this church a home to me.*

"I realized you don't have to live a perfect Christian life to be a person of faith," Paul Adams explained recently as he unlocked the church door for a weekend event. "But you do need to get in there and try to live it. It was these kids, these people, and seeing how they lived out their faith that brought me back to church and to faith in Christ. I mean, just look at me. Here I had determined to never darken the door of a church again. And now I have the key!"

Merry adds fervently, "The Karen here at All Saints have taught me what it means to be dedicated to God, dedicated to family, to forgive and pray even for those who have hurt you. Working with people of such faith and passion, it's impossible not to have it spill over on you."

Paul now began applying his love of reading to the Bible and other Christian literature. His days were so full helping with the Karen that he eventually retired from the IRS so he could give himself full time to his "real" job. He had never wanted to work with children, and Paul and Merry had never had children of their own. But now Paul found himself becoming an honorary grandpa to the younger Karen as Merry had become an honorary grandma.

To the Karen, the extended family is as close a tie as immediate siblings and parents. When one older Karen girl got married, Paul found himself invited up on the platform to join the father and other elder male relatives. Somewhat confused, he asked, "Whose daughter is she?"

"Your daughter," the girl's father told him. Father Bu Christ added, "All the Karen children are your children."

Paul and Merry Adams both could not agree more.

26

Kurios Farm was growing by leaps and bounds. Looking back over that first planting season, Michael could make a sizeable list of mistakes he especially had made. They'd overplanted some crops for what could be sold or used and under-planted others. Learning to drive a tractor and haul the water tank on its trailer without bulldozing the crops proved to be quite a challenge.

Still, despite Michael's own bumbling and ignorance of farming, God had blessed their efforts. By August, the first harvest was feeding those Karen attending All Saints and many others who didn't, as well as supplying Smyrna's Food Bank and the Salvation Army's own food drive. An Asian businessman who owned a chain of sushi counters and grocery stores purchased all the cucumbers. Volunteers helped sell the surplus at the Murfreesboro farm market.

But it was that strange crop over which Anglo volunteers had shaken their heads in bewilderment that provided the summer's greatest cash success. The sour leaf had grown into tall, bushy plants, a delicacy that would appear to be in such demand among Asian Americans that grocery chains were willing to pay three dollars a pound. The Kurios crop was quickly snapped up, and they could have sold far more.

In the end, Michael's expectations that farm proceeds would pay the church mortgage proved overly optimistic. But what it did accomplish was more than enough. They'd kept their commitment that the farm would take funds from neither diocese nor church. God had provided for all expenses through grants and gifts. The harvest had fed hundreds of people and netted at least a few thousand dollars. But beyond all that, the months of working side by side had bonded the two disparate parts of his All Saints congregation into a community as simply sharing the same sanctuary would never have done.

Snapshots of the summer filled Michael's mind. The younger and sturdier volunteers, Anglo and Karen, stooped over ripening cucumbers and squash. Merry deftly managing her power chair to catalogue produce. Aimee chatting with the older Karen women over the refreshment table, a brightly colored cooling ring around Aimee's neck, which permitted her to manage her MS symptoms in the outdoor heat. The bent heads of Landra Orr and Kathy Short as they examined a baby's rash or a child's fever. Michael Williams and Paul Adams discussing next week's ESL topic with Ye Win and Father Bu Christ. Atticus and Hadley racing across the green with the Karen children, playing some global version of hide-and-seek.

And the celebrations. The outdoor picnics and potlucks. They'd all learned to eat each other's food—spicy fish soup and pumpkin curry and meat-stuffed samosas, hamburgers, and hot dogs—and even to enjoy it. Yes, it had been a glorious summer. Kurios Farm had indeed become God's farm.

❊ ❊ ❊

There'd been other changes at All Saints. Harvest over, the beginning of winter offered opportunity for the entire congregation to rest and regroup. Landra Orr organized a Sunday school for the children, Karen teenagers helping to translate the Bible stories. The gift of a large church van from Trinity Episcopal Church in Winchester, Tennessee, meant that Ye Win no longer had to rise at five a.m. for the multiple car trips necessary to get many of the Karen to church.

Aimee was already leading a youth choir at St. Paul's in Murfreesboro. But bringing children and music together was second nature for Aimee, and she'd already noticed the beautiful voices of several Karen boys and girls. The Karen children appeared happy enough and to be adapting well. But Aimee occasionally glimpsed lostness and confusion in their eyes. How strange this all must seem to them. How disoriented they must feel in a world of babble they could not understand.

As clearly as Michael had known God was calling him to start a farm, Aimee knew God was calling her to give these children a voice of their own. And she knew only one way to do that. She neither spoke nor read Karen. But she'd recognized the melodies of several hymns they sang. One day after church, Aimee called the Karen children together, along with her own son, Atticus. First asking the Karen children to help her learn one of their hymns, she then taught them the English words for the same melody. Though they spoke little English, their gift for mimicry turned out to be as exceptional as their soaring, sweet voices. That first songfest grew into the All Saints children's choir, which would sing in both languages for offertories and special occasions.

The juxtaposition of two cultures could produce its humorous moments. One day Aimee decided it was time for her two choirs to socialize. So she invited the All Saints choir and the youth choir she taught at St. Paul's over to her house for a movie night. If the two groups of children couldn't understand each other enough to socialize, they were courteous enough. But Aimee soon noticed an odd huddle of Karen at the snack table, where she'd set out pizza and large bowls of bright-orange Cheetos.

Fifteen-year-old Ba Soh Wah was part of the group. Their whispered words were Karen, but their elbowed nudges, pointed fingers, and body language needed no interpretation. They were each daring the others to be the first to try those puffy worm-shaped objects covered with suspiciously bright-orange dust.

Finally, one boy stepped bravely forward. His look of wide-eyed astonishment followed by a beaming smile was all that was needed for the rest to dive in. By the evening's end, Aimee's All Saints choir was splattered in orange from their fingers to their mouths to their clothes.

"That was our first time to ever eat pizza or Cheetos," Ba Soh Wah remembers today. "We didn't think they would taste so good!"

With a twinkle in his eye and an exaggeration of his Tennessee drawl, Ba Soh Wah adds, "Now we Karen like to blame Miss Aimee for turning us all into junk food junkies!"

27

As 2008 drew to a close, not everyone at All Saints was happy with the changes. The All Saints congregation had traditionally sung the doxology every Sunday during the offertory. Since this wasn't part of the regular liturgy, Michael had felt no qualms at replacing it with such special music as the Karen children's choir. One woman had vociferously objected. She'd heard Michael out courteously when he'd tried to explain his reasoning, but shortly afterward, she stopped coming to church. When Michael gave her a call, she stated bluntly, "I'm not coming back."

"Is it because of the doxology?" Michael asked.

"No, I've just decided I want to go to church with people who look like me!"

Then there were the brass collection plates. If there was one area in which the Karen put the Anglo congregation to shame, it was that every Karen, down to the smallest toddler, brought some offering to put in the collection plate, even if it was just a dollar bill or a few coins. And however little they had, they were the first to give if a need was raised. One Sunday, Merry Adams asked for prayer for a friend, Debby, who had been diagnosed with cancer and could no longer work. She was stunned when the Karen immediately organized an offering, raising $250 to help with Debby's expenses.

Michael was surprised and concerned one Sunday when he

noticed that the brass collection plates used for the offering had been replaced with wicker baskets. The church council member in charge of handling the offerings was the same woman who'd sneered at Aimee's haircut and suggested she'd steal Aimee's husband if she were younger. When Michael asked her why they were no longer using the brass plates, the woman told him she was worried the Karen might steal them for the value of the metal, so she'd replaced them with baskets.

At Michael's insistence, she reluctantly restored the plates to use. But she continued to treat the Karen with disdain. Though by now she was well acquainted with their history, she would speak to them in her limited Spanish, and then look pained when they tried to explain that wasn't their language. Once the city stopped maintaining the ball fields, the grass needed to be cut. In a council discussion on whether to hire a grass-cutting service or find someone with time and equipment to donate, she demanded to know why the Karen weren't doing any needed lawn work. After all, weren't they getting plenty of handouts?

That the Karen were actually working hard at full-time jobs as well as volunteering with the farm, she brusquely dismissed. But the worst incident happened when an order came for a thousand pounds of sour leaf. At three dollars a pound, it would be the farm's first big payday. The downside was that the buyer was a full day's travel away in Colorado.

Volunteers cut the sour leaf, packed it into garbage bags, and loaded it into the church van. Then Ye Win drove the load all the way to Colorado. Unfortunately, the use of garbage bags was one more mistake born of inexperience. The airtight plastic caused the plants' moisture to condense inside so that by the time the load arrived, the sour leaf was badly wilted. The salvageable leaf brought only $1,000.

The church council member in question was furious when Ye Win brought the check back. "We were supposed to earn $3,000! This is what I'm talking about! These people are incompetent! This whole farm is a joke, a sham, just plain stupid!"

By now Michael had had enough. He had a well-earned reputation for calm. But his long-term friends knew that calm could
erupt if given enough impetus. And that impetus generally had
something to do with injustice, unfairness, or ungodliness. At this
moment, all three seemed in play.

"Now, just a minute!" he cut sternly into her tirade. "You talk
about what *we* are doing for those *people*, as you call them? You
wouldn't have a place to worship right now if those people hadn't
come. They saved your church for you. They've broken their backs
working out in the heat on that farm. Ye Win drove hundreds of
miles all the way up there to deliver that leaf—on his own time.
And even if things didn't go as well as we hoped, we're still $1,000
richer than a week ago. You should be on your knees, thanking
God for sending those people and for all they've done for this
church!"

Michael's response did nothing to change the council member's
attitude. She eventually came to Michael to express her disappointment in the direction All Saints had taken. "I had such hopes
for us here when you and Aimee came. For our congregation and
what we could become."

"What kind of hopes do you mean?" Michael asked.

"I was hoping to see these pews filled again. To have a vibrant
Sunday school and outreach into our community. For our church
to *be* something in this town again, like it used to be!"

Michael stared at her in disbelief. Just that Sunday, attendance
had been well over a hundred. The Sunday school was now so full
they needed more classroom space. He voiced his disbelief aloud.
"What are you talking about? Our attendance is now higher than
before the split. The pews are full. The Sunday school is overflowing with kids."

"I didn't mean with those people!" she snapped back instantly.

It was only at that moment that Michael realized how completely at cross-purposes their conversation was. To this woman,
the Karen simply weren't "real" church members. Her concept
for All Saints went back to her own 1950s youth when a "proper"

southern Episcopal congregation was not only Caucasian, but a bastion of upper class aristocracy.

Gently, Michael told her, "That's never going to happen here."

"Well, thank you for at least coming out and saying it," she replied. The next Sunday she was gone.

There was sorrow at her departure as well as for others who drifted away. But those who'd remained were there because they wanted to participate in what God was doing in their midst. They rejoiced in being part of the chaotic but warm, hospitable, and loving community that was now All Saints.

Another departure was far more painful. Ye Win's hectic schedule working full-time while ministering to Smyrna's growing Karen community left little time at home with the young bride who had once brought him a Bible in prison and accompanied him on a spousal visa to the United States. Ye Win had been aware she was not happy in this alien, cold new country. But she'd seemed happier once she accepted a position at Tyson Foods that no longer kept her cooped up in their small apartment.

Then in late 2008, the All Saints church council, the diocese, and the Karen community itself came together in recognition that Ye Win simply could not keep working full-time for both the Karen and his machinist job. Between the three groups, funds were found to hire Ye Win as a full-time lay worker at All Saints. For the first time in years, Ye Win could now enjoy an entire night's sleep and spend free hours with family. So it was a shock to come home one day to find that his wife of five years had packed up and left town with a co-worker. Ye Win poured his own grief into working even harder for the Karen community and All Saints congregation.

For the most part, the winter months passed peacefully. The congregation continued to grow. And All Saints found itself no longer defined by a bitter church split, but as the church that had been given new life and purpose through God's farm and God's farmers from halfway around the world. Reporters and news crews found their way to the church and its now-harvested vegetable plots. News write-ups followed, from regional Tennessee newspapers and TV stations to *USA Today* and Voice of America radio. A Los Angeles theater group and film producer read one article and was so moved by it that he called Michael to ask if All Saints would be willing to have their story turned into a movie.

Then the next planting season arrived. The All Saints congregation from young to old and even a number of community volunteers turned out to prepare the farmland for seed. They'd learned from the prior summer's mistakes, and this year sour leaf became the largest cash crop. Tomatoes, okra, zucchini, cabbage, and other crops were added to the squash, beans, cucumbers, lettuce, and radishes. Corn proved a failed experiment. But the tomatoes grew so abundantly, they almost rivaled the sour leaf.

From the church knoll, another new addition could be seen as well. Bo Ezell, an active longtime church member, wanted to create a memorial to his wife, who had served the diocese as the bishop's assistant for many years. Michael proposed an outdoor chapel on some of the bottomland still not plowed up for farming. This eventually became a gazebo, with stone altar and stone benches laid out at the center of walkways forming a mirror pattern of the cross that topped the church.

The stone benches and altar were placed facing east, and the chapel perimeter was sown with wildflowers. From then on, the Penny Ezell Chapel would be where the All Saints congregation gathered for Easter sunrise services and other special times of worship. Nearby, soccer goals had replaced softball backstops to provide the church youth with a playing field for "football," as the Karen called it.

When harvest arrived, volunteers converted a covered picnic pavilion adjacent to the church, but near the highway, into a market stand. There Merry Adams in her powered chair reigned supreme over sales. Special events such as a chef who came to do a cooking demo with Kurios Farm produce brought in visitors from nearby neighborhoods and as far away as Nashville. Merry Adams' original wish to be part of a community where she'd be recognized when stepping—or rather, wheeling—into the local grocery store had come true. All around town, complete strangers would come up to greet her. "Hey, you're the market lady from the farm of that church where they saved those refugees!"

"No, I'm from the church where those refugees saved us!" Merry would correct.

28

By Father Michael Spurlock's third year at All Saints, he could not have imagined being anywhere else. This was home. This was the mission to which God had called him. For which God had prepared him. His mind went back to what his friend Karl had said on that long-ago day when he'd been told of the decision to send him to Smyrna. "If you pull this off, Michael, you'll be a hero. But if you don't, no one will blame you because it's impossible!"

And they had pulled it off. Certainly not because Michael was any kind of hero. Nor, in fact, because of *anything* Michael had done. But because God had shown them mercy and grace and had reached down from heaven with miracle after miracle.

And now even the farm had accomplished its purpose and become less a necessity to the All Saints congregation and more a community project. The Karen were largely settled into jobs, schools, and new homes. Ye Win was no longer the only one with a driver's license. Nor the only one with English skills. The oldest Karen children were graduating from high school. Life at All Saints was no longer a battle for survival, but a new, accepted, placid normal.

But was Father Michael Spurlock the right person for All Saints' normal? What he had not shared with his congregation, nor even at first with Aimee, was a message that had been left on his answering machine one day late in August. It was from Father Andrew

Mead, rector of Saint Thomas Episcopal Church on Manhattan's Fifth Avenue.

Michael had met Father Mead briefly his first year of seminary. His only memories of that meeting were telling Father Mead how much he'd hated living in New York and how glad he'd been to leave. Now Father Mead was asking Michael to join him on staff at Saint Thomas.

"You were at the top of the list for recommendations," he'd joked when Michael called back. "But I was warned not to call you at home because if your wife knew that New York was calling, I might not get your true thoughts on the matter."

The two men talked on the phone for three hours. Michael found himself of one mind with Father Mead on every topic—theology, literature, their mutual love of Scripture. The position was, in fact, precisely what Michael had hoped for when he'd graduated from seminary—a staff position under a senior priest whom he deeply respected and who could help Michael grow in his priestly formation.

Nor did living in New York seem as unattractive as it once had. Atticus and Hadley were older now, and he and Aimee could see how their children could flourish in such an environment. And Aimee would be nearer to opportunities to use her experience in music and television to greater effect than in small-town Tennessee. Father Mead and Michael agreed to talk again in a few weeks. They both needed to pray and think.

There was a lot to pray about. Michael and Aimee were happy at All Saints. They'd seen so many miraculous happenings. They'd come to deeply love their congregation, both Anglo and Karen. So how could he even think of leaving All Saints when he was still so needed here?

Michael had once vowed to never "play" church. To give up all his own willfulness, ambitions, and desires to serve God alone. Did his attraction to Father Mead's offer mean that Michael was tempted to climb a ladder of prestige he'd vowed never to climb? Was he simply looking for a tidy escape from the admittedly hard, dirty work the last three years had entailed? More personally, did even considering such a move mean he was abandoning his flock?

When Michael and Father Mead next spoke in September, it was agreed that the Spurlocks would travel to New York in February to interview with Father Mead, his fellow clergy, and the wardens of the parish. Until that time, they would each reflect and pray to see if God might be calling Michael to Saint Thomas.

He and Aimee dedicated themselves to prayer. Aimee had already made it clear she'd be happy with whatever decision Michael made. What Michael wanted was a sign from God so definitive he'd know without a doubt God's choice for the Spurlock family.

No such overt sign came. But as Michael went about his duties, as he watched Ye Win growing spiritually in his new position, Father Bu Christ competently shepherding the Karen, Michael Williams, the Adamses, the Orrs, Kathy Short, and so many others selflessly meeting needs and taking on more and more of church responsibilities, he found his own perceptions changing.

One of Michael's favorite Bible quotes was from John the Baptist: "He [Christ] must increase, but I must decrease" (John 3:30). The miracle of All Saints had never been about Michael or anything he'd accomplished. It had always been about Jesus Christ, the beginning, the end, and the focus of this entire endeavor. So who was Michael to think All Saints could not move forward without his presence in perpetuity?

Michael was suddenly acutely aware that he was not the person God was calling to lead All Saints forward into the future. Perhaps he'd been the right person for those desperate times when All Saints had been at the end of their rope, about to lose everything they treasured as a church. If Michael had done one thing right, it had been to be attuned to hear when God spoke. But now was the season for All Saints to get down to normal, daily living, and God had not chosen Michael for that task. As Moses had stepped aside for his assistant Joshua, it was now time for Michael to hand off the wonderful privilege of shepherding this unique flock to whomever God had chosen for the next stage of their journey.

In February, as arranged, the Spurlocks traveled to New York City and Saint Thomas. It was near the end of their visit when Father Mead extended the call to Michael to join the staff at Saint Thomas Church, saying, "Trusting this is God's will . . ."

Without hesitation, Michael turned to Aimee. "What should I say?"

"Yes," Aimee responded, and Michael immediately echoed, "Yes."

When Michael returned home, he spoke to his bishop, then sat down to write his formal resignation letter to his parish. The next Sunday, he read it to the All Saints congregation. The aftershock was as difficult as he'd anticipated. The Karen were especially bewildered. Ye Win brought Michael their questions. "Is the bishop making you leave? Are they sending you away from us?"

That this was Michael's own choice was even harder for them to accept. Had they done something wrong that was driving him away? Did the Spurlocks no longer care about them?

All Michael's reassurances didn't help. The Spurlocks put their home on the market. Michael's last Sunday as vicar was scheduled to be May 9. One last time, he worked with Ye Win, Father Bu Christ, Christ Paw, Michael Williams, Paul and Merry Adams, and others to prepare and seed the fields for that summer's crops. Though he felt absolute peace that he'd made the right decision, he also felt that his heart was breaking. He wasn't sure what was worse—the loving farewell hugs from the Karen children or the unhappy, uncomprehending glances from their elders.

29

The spring of 2010 had already been one of the wettest on record in Smyrna. By the end of April, rivers were flooding throughout central Tennessee.

Then on Saturday, May 1, the skies opened up. By Sunday, the rainfall had doubled the area's previous record with more than thirteen inches falling within thirty-six hours. The Cumberland River, which flowed through Nashville, crested at more than fifty feet, with rivers throughout central Tennessee cresting as much as fourteen feet above prior records.

Downtown Nashville became a muddy brown lake rising to ten feet in depth. Residential streets and highways turned to raging rapids, inundating thousands of vehicles. The event was eventually termed a thousand-year flood, with one-third of Tennessee being declared a natural disaster zone. Though casualties were relatively few, less than thirty total, 10,000 families were displaced, while total property damages exceeded $2 billion.

Smyrna was no less affected. Like much of central Tennessee's rich bottomland, the twenty-two acres All Saints had purchased was designated floodplain. During their first planting season, Michael had asked if the creek ever flooded. Sure, he was told. In fact, in high water years, floodwaters had reached all the way to the bottom of the knoll on which the church stood. So Michael wasn't surprised when a church member called on Saturday, May 1, to warn him of quickly rising floodwaters below the church.

"We've just barely planted! What are we going to do if all our seed is washed away?" the panicked church member asked.

"I don't know," Michael answered. "But I'll drive out and take a look."

The torrential downpour lashed across the highway, turning the road into a rushing stream and cutting visibility so that Michael slowed to a crawl. Thankfully, the turnoff into the church drive was even a higher elevation than the knoll on which the church stood, so he reached the parking lot without difficulty. Sure enough, the freshly planted farm plots, chapel, and soccer field down below were now part of a single slow-moving river that had already covered the stone altar and benches. Even as Michael watched, the floodwaters rose to lap at the gazebo roof. The goalposts out on the soccer field were just visible poking out of the water.

But the river that flowed over Kurios Farm marked only the beginning. The rain continued through the night and the next day. When it finally stopped, Michael walked down the church hall to the back door. While he'd been prepared for further flooding, what he actually saw stunned him.

The river had swollen into a lake deep enough to cover the back door's concrete stoop. The market pavilion on its own knoll off to the left still stood intact above the water. But the windbreak of trees that edged the creek now showed only a few leafy branches thrusting out of the water on the far side of the lake. The gazebo, goalposts, a storage shed where the church kept farm equipment, the water tank on its trailer, the church's freshly planted crops—all had been swept away. If the water rose even a few more inches, the church would be flooded as well.

It was Monday before the rains finally stopped. The water was still rising, now lapping at the frame in which the back door hung. At least the parking lot and drive up to the highway were still above water. From inside the church, Michael waited for the flood to reach its peak. Would the floodwaters spill over to damage the church itself? The scene evoked another flood many millennia before. One that had wiped out all but eight survivors. After once having witnessed God's salvation of All Saints, was its destruction to be Michael's final legacy here?

But when the floodwaters crested Monday evening, not one drop had spilled over into the church building. The next morning, Michael stepped outdoors to see knoll and tree line beginning to emerge once again from the muddy lake that was the church property. Sunlight glinted along the crest of choppy brown waves.

Once again, the vista evoked that other long-ago flood. But this time it was not the thought of rising, destructive floodwaters that came to Michael's mind. It was God's promise to Noah and his family after the flood. A promise that never again would God send a flood that would wipe out all of humanity. Above the receding waters, God had set the sparkling prism of a rainbow as his everlasting sign that "while the earth remains, seedtime and harvest, cold and heat, winter and summer, and day and night shall not cease" (Genesis 8:22 NKJV).

"Seedtime and harvest . . . shall not cease!" This was the true message here, Michael realized. As that long-ago flood had not been the end for Noah and his family, neither would this one be the end for All Saints. Yes, the seed they'd sown had washed away. But they could replant. Michael was suddenly reminded of the day that conservation agency representative had come out to test their soil. The results showed some of the richest soil in Tennessee. In fact, it was the occasional flood depositing its nutrient-rich silt that made those acres so fertile.

"This land is made for farming," the representative had told Michael.

Yes, that was the literal truth. When God had spoken the world into creation, he had made this land to be perfect for growing food to feed his greatest creation, mankind. For countless millennia, it had sat virtually untouched and dormant. A family had briefly purchased the acres for farming. Then a church parish had acquired it, and once again it had sat fallow.

And God had watched over the land, as he'd been doing since he created it. He'd watched through the congregational split. He'd watched and waited for All Saints to make the slow turn from the pain of the past to hope for the future.

Were you waiting, God, to see if we were going to love you enough to be willing to walk away from those things to which a church can so easily become deeply attached? Were you waiting to see how far we were really willing to follow you? Or were you waiting until everyone thought we were dead and done for, so that when you brought us resurrection and new life everyone would recognize it was your doing and not ours?

And sure enough, in his own good time, God had brought together Michael Spurlock and his tiny struggling congregation with a group of farmers from the other side of the planet to once again put this land to use for its designed purpose of feeding hungry people. It all seemed such a messy, chaotic way to run a planet, Michael mused.

If man managed the deep workings of the world, I'm sure it would be a tidy sort of place, systematic, ordered in a human sort of way. But our ways would wind up starving it. To us, God's ways seem messier, chaotic. He lets the land lie fallow, floods it from time to time, covers it in mud and debris—and in the process makes it the richest farmland in the region. And I guess that applies to churches too. God's way is a lot messier and more unpredictable than I could wish. But he knows his business, and as the land thrives because of God's good purposes and provision, so do his people.

A deep peace settled over Michael. He would indeed leave. God would send his replacement. And the people of All Saints, Anglo and Karen, would continue forward, sowing seeds, harvesting crops, literally and spiritually. Floods might come again, as had happened this weekend. As had happened the day of that painful split. But the community of All Saints would just get back to work and plant again. Because that's what God's people did when the floods came.

In the following days, that was exactly what happened. As the floodwaters receded, the congregation turned out in force. The gazebo was rescued from the treetops and set back on its foundation. The stone altar and benches were scrubbed clean. The water tank was recovered downstream and restored to its location beside the creek. And the fields were replanted. The fall of 2010 would see Kurios Farm's biggest harvest yet.

By the next Sunday, May 9, cleanup efforts were well underway, not just at All Saints, but across central Tennessee. The All Saints sanctuary was packed as Father Michael Spurlock led the congregation in the familiar liturgy and celebrated the Eucharist one last time. In his sermon, he reviewed all that had happened at All Saints over the last three years.

It was a simple and familiar message. When the people are settled in the land, they should rehearse the mighty acts of God, teach them to their children, lest they forget the good things God has done for them. "Come and hear, all ye that fear God, and I will declare what he hath done for my soul" (Psalm 66:16).

God's greatest work at All Saints? Transforming two groups of strangers from opposite sides of the planet at first into fellow laborers, then into friends, then into one family. By the time he finished, Michael was weeping right alongside his people.

30

A nd then it was over. Good-byes said, Michael and Aimee, with Atticus and Hadley, packed up their things and moved to New York. By the time the reseeded fields were sprouting green shoots, a new vicar had been appointed to All Saints, Father Randy Hoover-Dempsey.

An ordained Presbyterian minister, Randy had left the pastorate to teach for the following twenty years in Nashville's public school and university system. At that time he and his wife, Kathy, were attending St. Bartholomew's Episcopal Church in Nashville, where Randy served as a lay leader, leading prayer meetings and doing hospital visitation. The couple had raised three children and were enjoying eight grandchildren when Randy felt called to return to ministry in 2004, at the age of fifty-seven. Two years later, he received his ordination in the Episcopal Church.

St. Bartholomew's had become host to a large community of refugees from southern Sudan, the majority of Christian heritage from the Dinka tribe. Many of the young men were former "lost boys," kidnapped as children by rebel warlords and forced to fight their brutal battles. Those at St. Bartholomew's were the fortunate ones who'd managed to escape to a refugee camp, then to the United States.

When Randy was asked if he would serve as liaison to the Sudanese congregation, he was immediately interested. As a child, Randy had devoured biographies of missionaries such as Albert

Schweitzer, medical missionary to Africa. The St. Bartholomew congregation had prayed for and supported ministries and missionaries in Africa. Now God was bringing African ministry to their door. Unlike All Saints, the Sudanese held their own separate services, but Randy worked closely with their leadership, setting up ESL and other programs, helping those serving in ministry to apply for scholarships to seminary.

Then in 2009, Randy was asked to serve as interim pastor in a small church two hours south of Nashville. For the next year, he commuted twice a week. That church had just called a full-time rector when Randy received a phone call from the bishop. Father Michael Spurlock, vicar of All Saints, was moving to New York. Randy had experience working with refugees. Would he consider replacing Father Michael at All Saints?

For Randy, what he would consider was not the question. If the bishop needed him at All Saints, he would go. The opportunity to work with a multicultural congregation again was a plus, and after the long commute of the past year, the location was an easy drive from his Nashville home.

August 1, 2010, was Randy's first Sunday as vicar of All Saints, and if the congregation still mourned the Spurlocks' departure, it was immediately apparent that All Saints and Father Randy Hoover-Dempsey belonged together. Members who'd been there from the beginning of All Saints still tell stories of Father Randy's arrival. After his first service, he'd asked the church council, "Do all these people understand English?"

By the next Sunday, Father Randy had arranged with Ye Win and others for simultaneous translation of his sermon and all other parts of the service. He searched out translations of Karen hymns, so that all singing in the services could be done in both languages. Among the songs he searched out was "Jesus Loves Me," which became a standard part of the service, sung when the children went forward to partake in the Eucharist.

Randy also quickly recognized that the Karen ranged widely from those like the Kunoo and Bu Christ families, who were highly educated, to others who could barely read or write in any language. During his teaching career, Randy had worked many years with elementary-age students, and he used the same techniques of illustrations, props, and stories to make his sermons both fun and comprehensible across the language and education barrier.

"I credit Ye Win for improving on my sermons," Randy Hoover-Dempsey remembers with a smile. "He refused to translate my jokes if they weren't funny in the Karen language. In truth, the key to everything that happened at All Saints while I was there was Ye Win. He has the greatest pastoral heart of anyone I've met. It was his doing that people were actually lining up to be part of All Saints."

And indeed, the church was once again growing rapidly. In Father Randy's first year, attendance had topped 180 with 225 on special occasions. The children's Sunday school had almost 100 children, most of them Karen. A church family donated a beautifully carved stone baptismal font. By the end of his six years at All Saints, Father Randy had officiated at more than 100 baptisms. In fact, the church became so crowded, even with extra chairs brought in to line aisles and back, that a second service was started. But Father Randy quickly discovered that the Karen preferred to worship together as one community, however overcrowded, than to split up, so the second service was dropped.

Because the Eucharist was so familiar to both Anglo and Karen congregants, it became increasingly central to the worship. The children would pour forward first, singing "Jesus Loves Me" in both languages, to receive a blessing, or Communion if they were old enough to have received baptism. Then the adults would file left and right to kneel at the altar, intermingled irrespective of ethnicity, where they would receive the elements from Father Bu Christ in Karen or Father Randy in English.

The Karen children, in turn, remember Father Randy as the priest who sang with them and joined in their games. Randy's wife, Kathy, also found herself immediately at home at All Saints. She became known as the church photographer. For every church occasion, she took hundreds of pictures, posting them on bulletin boards along the church hallway. The children and youth especially would crowd around each Sunday to pick out their own faces among the photos.

"This church needed Michael Spurlock so desperately when he came," shares one long-term Anglo church member. "If not for Michael, this church would not be here. The Karen wouldn't be here. Michael did what God called him to do here. But if it were not for Randy and Kathy Hoover-Dempsey, All Saints would not have continued to survive. They were what we needed for the next phase of our church."

The other outreach activities Michael had initiated continued on. The crops were harvested. That next spring, they were again sown. ESL classes. Tutoring. Transportation. Free clinics at the church. Help filling out paper work and dealing with government, school, and medical bureaucracies. All of these ebbed and flowed according to need.

"We tried to carry on what Michael Spurlock started," Randy Hoover-Dempsey explains. "And to give Ye Win support in what he was doing as leader in his community."

Like Michael Spurlock, Father Randy also made clear that he considered Father Bu Christ his equal in church leadership, inviting him always to participate in administering Eucharist and other parts of the worship service as well as minister among his own Karen people. Father Randy also facilitated an ongoing relationship between the All Saints congregation and the Spurlocks in New York. His first August in New York, Michael invited Ye Win to share his story with the youth of Saint Thomas. The next summer, Michael brought his youth group to All Saints to help with Kurios Farms, establishing a playground for the children and assisting with a sour leaf harvest.

The relationship with All Saints has also opened up doors for ministry in Myanmar itself, including helping fund a vehicle for the Hpa-an diocese in Karen territory where Father Bu Christ and John Kunoo once preached the gospel. And for both the Spurlocks and the All Saints congregation, especially the Karen, the ongoing interchange healed much of the pain of the Spurlocks' departure.

Much later, Ye Win explained to Michael, "We couldn't understand why you left. We thought you didn't care about us anymore. Or that you were running away from us because we were too much trouble. But then you kept in touch. You didn't just disappear. We realized that you still cared about us. Even though you were far away, we could call you if we had a need, and we are still in relationship with one another."

A relationship the Spurlocks continue to count dear. *This is the beauty of the body of Christ,* Michael could now see. *Even when separated by geography and time, we are still one community, one family. I will count myself privileged to call Ye Win, Father Bu Christ, John Kunoo, Christ Paw, Paul and Merry Adams, Bo Ezell, Michael Williams, and all the others at All Saints as my friends, and brothers and sisters, until we meet the Lord.*

31

Karen families were beginning to contact the church from other cities, asking if they could move to Smyrna to attend All Saints. With Ye Win now working full-time at the church, he was free to travel to help families move. Ye Win remained busy helping new families find housing, furniture, clothes, and jobs. But now many others were volunteering alongside him. In 2011, God brought a new blessing to Ye Win's life: marriage to a beautiful and godly young woman, Pa Lay Paw. Over the following four years, three children would be born to them: Joshua Glory, Felicity, and Solomon.

※ ※ ※

But not all newcomers were Karen. An air force veteran, Bob Druecker had served with the US Department of Justice. After retirement, he'd become an educational assistant for the Smyrna school district. Fluent in Spanish, he'd expected to work with that language group. Instead, he was asked if he'd be willing to help tutor refugee students from a number of countries across Asia and the Middle East, including the Karen.

It was his granddaughter, Ciarra Black, who introduced Bob to All Saints. The two teenage daughters of All Saints member Tyler Mann, Annalise and Andrea, were among volunteers helping tutor Karen children. One evening they'd brought along their friend Ciarra. Barely into her own teens, Ciarra became one of the program's most devoted volunteers and was soon insisting her grandfather come meet some of the same students he was working with in the school system.

Bob's first stint teaching ESL classes at All Saints was shortly after the arrival of Father Randy in 2010. Though raised attending church, he'd turned his back on religion at age seventeen when he joined the military. But something about this particular group of refugees tugged at his heart. They'd been through so much. For one Karen teenager, her mother and one brother were the only survivors of her family. When the Burmese military had burnt their village, her mother had pleaded with the soldiers to spare their crops so the family would not starve. Instead, the soldiers had shot her father and other siblings, then sneered, "Now you won't need so much food!"

Another girl had been smuggled over the border as a toddler in a backpack, her mouth taped shut to keep her cries from tipping off roaming soldiers. Almost every child there evinced some kind of trauma. So much of their new life bewildered them. But they also evidenced a strong faith in the very God on whom Bob had turned his back. And both the children and their parents seemed to care about him as much as he'd come to care about them.

One Sunday, Bob decided to see for himself what was drawing them to this particular church. Sunday after Sunday, he returned. It was not an overnight change, but his personal faith began to grow. So did his involvement at All Saints. He tutored children in their homework, helped adults negotiate the process of citizenship, provided transport to medical appointments, even used his law enforcement experience to deal with occasional family conflicts. God had called him to this, Bob realized. One day he called an acquaintance who was a minister in New York.

"What do I have to do to become a missionary?" he queried.

"What are you doing now?" the acquaintance asked him.

When Bob explained, his acquaintance assured him firmly, "You're already a missionary."

"I always wondered if angels really exist," Bob shares today.

"Then I met these Karen kids, and I realized, yes, they do! Through these kids, God brought me back to himself. Back to what is true love. That's real miracle stuff!"

❋ ❋ ❋

Another newcomer, Lisa Lehr grew up Catholic and over her lifetime attended virtually every Protestant denomination. But by the time she moved to Smyrna, she was no longer attending any church. Eventually she made an agreement with her housemate, who was a Christian and did attend church, to find a church home. All Saints Episcopal Church was only a mile from her home, so in the spring of 2014, Lisa decided to give it a try. She was pleasantly surprised to worship in two languages and felt immediately welcomed by both the Karen and Anglo members.

A few weeks later, on Palm Sunday, the worship service included a celebratory parade around the church with everyone singing "We Are Marching in the Light of God" while waving palms. At one point, Lisa steadied herself by putting her hand on the shoulder of a Karen woman in front of her. Behind her, a tiny older Karen woman put her own hand on Lisa's shoulder. While she had no idea who the older woman was, when the procession came to an end, the woman gave Lisa a big hug. To Lisa, it was like a wave of welcome and love sweeping over her. She had found her church home.

Lisa was soon involved in many aspects of All Saints' church life, including Vacation Bible School (VBS) and Sunday school. Her work experience included Christian publishing and curriculum, which she soon applied to this unique community. One VBS program she wrote, *Fun on the Farm*, was developed with Kurios Farm in mind. A garden plot was dug up just for the children, who delighted in planting their own crops. The lessons, which Lisa led along with Landra Orr and Karen volunteers, all centered on sowing, reaping, and harvesting. Even lunchtime and crafts centered around the farm theme, including having the kids create recipes with pudding, cookies, and candy to make "rocky," "sandy," and "good" soil the children could actually eat.

The next year, Lisa wrote another VBS program for the church, *A Celebration of God's Love*, focusing on biblical celebrations, including the prodigal son's welcome home feast and the Palm Sunday parade, each lesson containing both Karen and Anglo cultural elements. For Lisa, it was a celebration as well of her own homecoming to a church and family that had indeed become home.

❋ ❋ ❋

While Karen congregants typically found their way to All Saints through community and family ties, Father Randy was beginning to note a significant pattern among new Anglo members. They came with a yearning for fellowship and community. For genuine faith. For a mission to serve others.

And somehow, they were finding all of these at All Saints. The Karen would be the first to admit they were not angels by any definition. They weren't the dangerous aliens some locals considered all refugees to be, nor saintly heroes for simply having survived. They were, in fact, ordinary, flawed humans. When some of the pre-split congregants of All Saints accused the Karen of joining a church of sinners, their response was unequivocal: "Yes, we are sinners. But Jesus came for sinners. He helped us. He redeemed us."

Visitors often found the exuberance of worship, the untidiness of two-way translation, and the participation of children at the Eucharist and throughout the service to be an overwhelming experience. They also found the warm hospitality and communal culture of the Karen. They were either drawn to the experience, or they enjoyed it as a tourist might a trip to Westminster Abbey, then looked elsewhere for a church home.

Which was fine with Father Randy. All were welcome at All Saints. But it was those who felt called to become part of this unique community, to pour themselves into ministry to the Karen and others in need, that All Saints needed as long-term members.

32

B y this time Karen sat on the All Saints church council, and at least half of church expenses were being covered by their offerings. Father Randy had been praying as well for someone to oversee the farm, an area in which he had zero experience. Both Anglo and Karen church members continued to volunteer, but they had jobs and increasingly busy lives of their own. Then David and Annetta McGee moved from Baton Rouge, Louisiana, to Smyrna and began attending All Saints.

David had been an agricultural major in college and had recently retired from an engineering career. Back in Baton Rouge, he'd overseen a community garden project. Now he took on oversight of Kurios Farm, which included mentoring both Karen and Anglo volunteers in modern agricultural techniques as well as spending more time on the tractor, plowing and harrowing, than anyone else in the church. Productivity continued to climb until more food was being produced than could be sold or given away.

That very first summer, Michael Spurlock had discussed the farm's future with Michael Williams: "There's going to be a time when we don't need the farm anymore. Or at least not in the same way. Will we be able to lay it down and do what is best for the next generation? Ten years from now, we don't want to be known as the farming church if no one has any idea anymore why we're doing it!"

Sure enough, as the years went by, as food and jobs were no longer so scarce, as families moved further away and teenagers

181

went off to college, Kurios Farm became less central to church activities and identity. Instead of a joint effort, the church now offers garden plots to any family with time and interest to farm. Surplus is given away to local food pantries and anyone in need.

Still, finances remained an issue. One day when funds were short for a needed project, Ye Win suggested All Saints install a "God-box." Father Randy was immediately intrigued. "What on earth is a God-box?"

Ye Win explained. A God-box was common in Karen churches. When God brought a special blessing into their lives, Karen Christians would drop an extra offering into the God-box to give thanks.

A charming custom, Father Randy concurred, but not for an American church like All Saints. For over a year, Father Randy dismissed the idea. But when the Karen continued to bring it up, at last a God-box was crafted and installed. Once a quarter, its contents were emptied to add to the weekly offering. The first time the box was emptied Father Randy was stunned to count up $4,000.

"I've learned my lesson," he told Ye Win. "Next time you give me an idea, I'm going to listen more quickly. We could have solved our financial problems if I'd just listened to you from the first!"

And in fact, Father Randy was amazed at the giving spirit of the Karen Christians. Too many locals saw the Karen and other refugees as simply a drain on resources, taking rather than contributing. But despite their admittedly limited resources, the Karen at All Saints came together to give sacrificially whenever they saw a need.

One such unexpected blow to church finances was when the magnificent round stained-glass window at the rear of the sanctuary, which showcased the victorious Lamb of God from the book of Revelation, began to crumble from its frame. To fix it would cost $15,000. When the need was announced, Ye Win's wife, Pa Lay Paw, quietly made the rounds of the Karen community, collecting a total of $8,000 toward the window.

Communal solutions were how the Karen dealt with every problem. And there were problems, many of them. Social workers and mental health professionals who have dealt with the Karen refugee community have diagnosed accurately some degree of PTSD for all the adult refugees as well as many of the children, especially the older teens. Not all have turned to faith in Jesus Christ nor had a strong family or church support network. Too many have turned to drugs and alcohol to deal with psychological trauma.

Local drug dealers and gangs sought to recruit Karen youth, sometimes successfully. Within the low-income apartment projects, where ten or more often lived in apartments designed for four, gang members would show up waving MAC-10s and other semiautomatics to demand protection payments. Afraid for their families, Karen men, many of them former guerrilla fighters, began arming themselves with rifles and shotguns.

Father Randy invited the police chief to church. The police chief came, took part in the worship service, and then addressed the congregation with Ye Win translating for him. "We are your police force," he made clear. "We are here to help you. If you feel threatened in any way, simply call 9-1-1. You don't have to give your names. Simply say the word *Chalet*, and we'll send a unit out to help you."

The police chief also arranged for more frequent police patrols within the low-income neighborhoods. It was the beginning of a mutually supportive relationship between the Karen community and the local police. The number of confrontations dropped dramatically.

They continued to drop as the years went on, simply because the Karen were becoming integrated into the community. They moved into homes of their own. Father Randy was kept busy participating in "home blessings" for each new move. These typically involved a hundred or more Karen crowded into the new house for a worship service. Accommodating so many was simple, since spread-out rugs and blankets provided for Karen-style seating with actual chairs and sofas reserved for Anglo guests. Father Randy and Father Bu Christ would then pray a blessing over each room in the house as well as the family, followed by a feast of spicy Burmese dishes.

The food proved Father Randy's one obstacle in integrating

with his Karen congregation. He loved the taste, but the spice and heat were just too much for his Tennessee-bred stomach. Typically, the Karen took note without criticism. At the next house blessing, a plate piled high with pepperoni pizza slices graced the table along with the curries and chili-redolent soups. That allowance to Anglo guests became a tradition at All Saints Karen gatherings that continues to this day.

❊ ❊ ❊

In contrast, Paul Adams had developed a taste for spicy food during his globe-trekking years in the navy. In fact, he'd earned local fame for the fiery sweetness of his chicken wings. The Adams home had become an open door for the church youth. Always on the lookout for new teaching topics, Paul held a few sessions on cooking American food. The Karen youth in turn would contribute their own spicy snack favorites, fiery-hot samosas or sweet-and-salty coconut rice balls.

Their eagerness to learn gave Paul an idea that could help them absorb the American concepts of marketing and sales. Using tomatoes and other produce from their own church farm, Paul worked with the teens to adapt family recipes and seasoning combos into a variety of unique hot sauces and salsas. "Old Sailor" soon became a hot local product line, especially since it was anyone's guess when a new batch would be available.

But if the Karen teens learned how to calculate costs and profits and do marketing promotions, as well as techniques of bottling and canning, it wasn't to fill their own pockets. "Old Sailor" became their mission project. Their first proceeds bought a new carpet for the church nursery. Other revenues went to the Nashville Rescue Mission and other charities.

The mortgage remained the single largest burden hanging over the All Saints congregation's collective heads. Though the initial idea of the farm providing funds to cover that debt had never materialized, the miracle Michael had witnessed in his first year at All Saints continued. Regardless of expenses, regardless of total offerings, that $10,000 the diocese had given to put All Saints back on its feet somehow was never depleted.

Part of God's provision was an ongoing drop in interest rates, so that the monthly payments on the loan gradually dropped from $5,500 to $3,000 to around $1,500 a month. Still, all the math said that their $10,000 should long since have been used up time and time again. While not yet self-sufficient, All Saints had metamorphosed from the poorest, smallest church in the Tennessee diocese to its fastest-growing congregation. Each local church tithed its own income to the diocese, and in 2011, the diocese came together to pay off the All Saints mortgage as a mission project.

"Every time a need arose, we'd wonder how we'd meet it," Father Randy remembers. "And somehow we always did. It sure wasn't because All Saints had some great strategy or we were good planners. It was simply because the church community came together and God answered prayers time after time after time."

33

It was not simply upkeep of their church that brought the All Saints community together. Psychological traumas were not the only health issues the Karen refugees had brought with them across the ocean. One of the original All Saints congregants and council members, Kathy Short, was a professional social worker who dealt routinely with Medicare and Medicaid. Paul Adams had been a medic during his decades in the navy. Together, they set up a health care program at All Saints, including free clinics at the church itself, as well as helping the Karen negotiate the health system.

Finding dentists willing to donate services to deal with countless rotting and missing teeth was difficult enough. But the Karen weren't used to turning to doctors for less than life-or-death situations. One church mother had lost all sight in one eye, and the other was deteriorating, when her palsied tremors were noticed while she was taking Communion. Father Randy's wife, Kathy, had taught at Vanderbilt University in Tennessee, whose medical school maintained a free clinic and other pro bono health care. All Saints volunteers rushed the mother to the medical school, where it was discovered she had a brain tumor the size of a tennis ball pressing down on her eye socket. The medical school admitted the Karen mother without charge, and thanks to immediate surgery, her sight was restored.

But not long afterward, the same woman's daughter, April Paw, grew ill. One of the top students among the Karen refugee children, the nine-year-old had been hiding her symptoms for fear she might be prohibited from attending school. But her jaundiced condition soon became so apparent that Ye Win insisted on driving her to the Vanderbilt teaching hospital emergency room. The news was distressing. April had a rare degenerative kidney disease. So rare, symptoms were often missed. Her attending doctor turned out to be the country's top expert on the disease. That was the first miracle.

The bad news was that April urgently needed a kidney transplant. In fact, if they hadn't discovered the disease, April would have been dead within months. As it was, April began a lengthy hospital stay. The only time she broke down in tears was when she learned she would not be able to return to school that year. She eventually received a transplant, but her body rejected the donated kidney. If another one was not found, she could not survive long on dialysis. Even more discouraging, April's refugee status provided no health care benefits for a second transplant.

Then her older brother Eh Htoo, seventeen years old at the time, discovered that once he turned eighteen, he could volunteer as a donor. When his birthday came, he went in for testing. The results showed that he would be an excellent match. There were still no funds for surgery, but the Vanderbilt teaching hospital agreed to do the surgery free of charge. A Christian medical ministry, Siloam Health Care, stepped in to help with physician's care and prescription costs.

The All Saints congregation now sprang into action. One group headed up by Kathy Short was designated Team April, their responsibility to drive April and her family back and forth, help monitor all the pre-op and post-op care, deal with paper work, find volunteers to translate for the doctors, ensure the family understood all instructions. A second group headed by Paul Adams formed Team Eh Htoo, to carry out the same process with April's older brother. Even such issues as drinking a precise amount of water to protect both donated and remaining kidneys needed to be monitored, as well as learning new routines necessary to live long-term with one kidney.

April had been given her name because she was born in April, and her surgery ended up scheduled for April 15. The transplant proved successful, and both siblings healed well. When it was over, Paul Adams joked with Eh Htoo, "So what are you going to get your sister for her birthday next year? Kind of hard to top this one!"

Eh Htoo just grinned, brushing off any suggestion that his act of love and sacrifice was anything out of the ordinary. Though she will always have to monitor her condition, April is now a healthy teenager who remains at the top of her classes in high school and whose fluent English gives little indication she was born in a refugee camp on the other side of the planet.

After this experience, Siloam Health Care began donating time and a nurse for regular clinics at All Saints, under the administration of Paul Adams as parish health care coordinator and Kathy Short as health care assistant, a program that has benefitted not only All Saints congregants but hundreds of others. No one in need of help is turned away.

Those at All Saints with proficiency in social bureaucracies have not been shy about jumping in to defend their Karen family. One Karen mother called Merry Adams for help with her middle-school son, since Merry had extensive legal aid experience. The son was virtually blind and failing in the mainstream public school. The mother had tried to enroll her son in the School for the Blind. The middle school superintendent insisted the boy didn't have sufficient English skills.

When Merry accompanied the mother to an arbitration meeting, the superintendent was furious. A mother could invite along anyone she wanted, Merry pointed out. The supervisor pulled out test scores to prove the boy wouldn't be able to handle language requirements at the blind school. He added, "In any case, what could they teach him that we can't? After all, we've supplied him a cane."

"Can you teach him to pour hot coffee, to differentiate money, to read Braille?" Merry challenged furiously. "In any case, what is the date on those test results?"

The superintendent reluctantly admitted they dated from a year prior, shortly after the boy had first entered the middle school's ESL program. Even more furious, Merry demanded, "Are you suggesting this boy hasn't learned any more English in the past year? This is not acceptable! We demand this meeting be rescheduled so that his ESL teacher can be brought in to testify to his current English proficiency. Which happens to be more than adequate to pass entrance requirements at the blind school!"

At the next meeting, the transfer was approved, and the boy, now a young man, is thriving in his new academic environment. Another score for Team All Saints.

The school system was not the only hurdle where the refugee population faced routine hostility. On another occasion, one of the older Karen teens had saved wages to purchase a car. The dealer sold him the car but told him that paper work for the title was not yet ready. Three months later, he had been given excuse after excuse as to why he had still not received the title. The teen finally asked Paul Adams for help. Dressing formally in tie and sports jacket, Paul accompanied the youth to ask in person for his title papers.

"It's already been mailed," the woman behind a customer service desk insisted. "Or maybe it's been filed at our other location. You will have to wait while we check."

Paul Adams simply stood beside the teen without saying a word. But the woman's excuses trailed off as she took in his tall, broad-shouldered bulk and military stance. Falling silent, she rooted around and within moments had come up with the title.

But Paul Adams' greatest satisfaction has been in helping Karen families through the citizenship process. In his first weeks teaching ESL at All Saints, he'd seen eyes light up as he'd explained the Constitution and what it meant to be an American citizen. Now his own eyes filled with joyful tears as he witnessed those same students take their oath of citizenship.

For the Adamses, it has been a joint effort. While Merry helped fill out forms, Paul would drive his former students to have their fingerprints taken or to citizenship interviews. The older Karen especially needed plenty of tutoring for English comprehension and civics tests. Naturalization ceremonies are carried out at the federal courthouse in Nashville just opposite the Episcopal cathedral. Paul Adams has attended every ceremony he can, cheering as his Karen students stand with over fifty others from countries all over the world to state their country of origin, then proudly recite the Pledge of Allegiance and take the oath of citizenship.

"These are people who left important jobs as teachers, judges, farmers," reminds Paul Adams, "who came eight thousand miles to work night shifts at Tyson so their children could have a better future. Just remember, these people are going to be the future of America, and if you ask me, that future is looking good!"

In 2016, Father Randy and Kathy Hoover-Dempsey were both past retirement age and feeling the need to spend more time with their own growing flock of grandchildren. Once again, leaving All Saints was difficult for them as well as the congregation. And once again, God had already chosen the right shepherd to step into Father Randy's shoes. Father Robert Rhea was an ER doctor who had left private practice and gone back to seminary to become a bi-vocational priest. His wife, Lisa, was a gifted musician and harpist. Under their loving care, the cycle of seedtime and harvest, births and graduations, house blessings and church festivals, joys celebrated and sorrows comforted, continued unbroken at All Saints.

34

On Sunday, October 2, 2016, the Spurlock family returned to Smyrna to worship together with the All Saints congregation for the first time since moving back to New York. The occasion was to celebrate a story of God's faithful provision that had somehow never died away.

Periodically over the years, news crews had turned up at All Saints to see what was happening with that odd little church saved by a group of refugee farmers from across the ocean. While Michael Spurlock was still vicar at All Saints, a Los Angeles film producer had read an article on the miracle of Kurios Farm and approached Michael about turning the All Saints story into a movie. After the Spurlocks' move to New York, the producer, Steve Gomer, had kept in touch, occasionally revisiting the idea.

Growing up in Yonkers, New York, Steve Gomer had always loved theater. He'd attended State University of New York's Purchase School of the Arts and worked as production coordinator for Circle Repertory Company before heading to Hollywood, where he'd produced and directed such movies as the Sundance award-winning film *Fly by Night*, *Sweet Lorraine*, and *Barney's Great Adventure*. He also directed countless television episodes for *Blue Bloods*, *Grey's Anatomy*, *Gilmore Girls*, *Private Practice*, *Without a Trace*, *Heartland*, and other prime-time TV series.

So what would impel a secularist from New York City of Jewish heritage to produce a movie about a southern Christian church?

Steve explains, "To me, it's about community and faith. We live in really troubled times and in such a polarized, divisive world. What sustains us is having community. And faith in God, because there is no denying the providential hand of God in what happened at All Saints."

To Steve Gomer, the miracle of All Saints was a parallel to what he sees as God's providential hand in bringing together the All Saints movie itself. One such instance was finding the right scriptwriter for the project. Steve Gomer had been invited to speak at University of Southern California (USC), home of one of the country's top film programs. Steve mentioned to a contact there that he was looking for a scriptwriter.

"Well, our best writer is a man named Steve Armour," Steve was told. "He's a bit older than our typical student. In fact, he was a prominent jazz musician but always wanted to write, so he went back to school on scholarship."

The description immediately interested Steve Gomer, since Michael Spurlock had also changed professions later in life, and was both a writer and a musician. He arranged a lunch meeting with Steve Armour to discuss the project. A tall, lanky man in his thirties, the other Steve jumped in with both feet. "I know the story of All Saints. I guess you're interested in me because I'm from the South. Grew up in Alabama, just south of Smyrna, in fact."

Startled, Steve Gomer responded, "Well, no, in fact, I didn't know, but we do need someone who knows the South."

"Oh, okay. Then it's my Christian faith and the fact that my father was a minister of a church, just like Michael Spurlock."

"No, I didn't know that either," Gomer admitted. "But you're checking off too many boxes on my list here to be coincidence. I think it's clear that you are the right person to write this movie."

In writing the script itself, both Steves struggled with finding an appropriate ending. The true-life actuality of bountiful harvests and a growing church made a happy, but hardly dramatic, ending. Since the movie had of necessity been fictionalized to some extent, they discussed perhaps changing the ending to something more inspiring. Maybe a flood to threaten crops and challenge the fictional congregation's trust in God. Perhaps even conclude with an ultimate challenge of faith, such as Father Michael leaving All Saints.

Steve Gomer picked up the phone to see what Michael Spurlock might think of such a departure from fact. Michael's first words left him stunned. "Steve, I was just going to call you. I wanted to let you know we're leaving All Saints. In fact, this next Sunday is our last here. We wanted to invite you to join us. Oh, and you may have seen on the news the thousand-year flood that hit central Tennessee this last week. Let me tell you what God has done here at the church."

Once again, Steve Gomer was left shaking his head. You could call this the century's biggest coincidence or God's hand of providence. Steve Gomer had no doubt which it was. Both Steves immediately booked a flight out, arriving in time to attend Father Michael's last service as vicar of All Saints.

But a script was not a movie, and finding funds to produce and distribute a faith-based film was not easy in the best of times. Over the next years, the project was tabled time and time again, but Steve Gomer refused to give up on it. By now, he'd become close friends with the Spurlocks and traveled many times to visit the All Saints congregation.

Steve and his wife, Jane, were sharing a meal with Ye Win and his family when they glanced across the table at each other, instantly recognizing they were sharing the same thought. This meal, this home, was like stepping back to the time when their own great-grandparents had arrived in the United States from Russia, refugees fleeing religious and ethnic persecution, struggling to learn a new language and a new alphabet. Community and faith had helped them not only survive but flourish. Now here were the Karen, leaving behind homeland, language, even alphabet, but sustained as their own families had been by community and their church.

And as in All Saints' own story, every time Steve Gomer was ready to throw in the towel, something would happen that could be seen as nothing less than the hand of God that kept the project going. When he finally realized the only way to complete the movie would be to quit his day job, move to Tennessee, and dedicate himself full-time to the project, his own rabbi contributed the funds for the move. Then Sony Affirm films agreed to distribute the movie if funds could be raised for production. Christian ministries and church organizations with a burden for refugees committed to raising some of the production costs.

"Every time we were in despair," Steve Gomer remembers now, "something would come along to lift our spirits and say we've got to keep going."

And so the first weekend of October 2016, Steve Gomer, Steve Armour, and a full film cast, including Emmy Award and Golden Globe nominee John Corbett (*My Big Fat Greek Wedding I/II, Northern Exposure*), Cara Buono (*Stranger Things, Mad Men*), Nelson Lee (*Law & Order*), Christian comedian Chonda Pierce, Barry Corbin, and David Keith, joined together with the real-life All Saints congregation for the filming of the movie *All Saints*.

"In the end, the story of All Saints became my own journey too," Steve Gomer shares today. "When I went into this, I didn't have a personal faith. I believed in God, but that was about it. When I met Michael, he talked so openly about God. He told me I needed to start praying every day. I have, and it has really given me great sustenance.

"I've seen God's hand so unmistakably in this remarkable story. Not a story of kindhearted Americans saving poverty-stricken refugees from some Third World country, but a story of coming together through God's working, and by their coming together creating a community that has brought salvation from and to both sides."

Steve adds, "There is truly something so compelling about this story that I feel privileged to be a small part of it, to have gotten to know and become friends with Michael, Aimee, and all the people at All Saints. I have grown as a person, as a human being, certainly in my faith, through this journey. It has changed me."

35

For the Spurlocks, the years in New York City had been good ones. In his current assignment of pastoral care, Michael had found his calling. The congregation at Saint Thomas ranged from the city's wealthiest to its most poor and needy, along with the countless tourists who wandered in to listen to the boys' choir sing choral services and concerts. Michael simply saw a lot of people who desperately needed to know Jesus Christ. While his first congregation would always hold a special place in his heart, he'd found peace at Saint Thomas and certainty that this was where God had called him for this season.

But arriving at All Saints still felt like a homecoming for each of them. They found the All Saints grounds in upheaval. What had been the soccer field to the lower right was filled with film production trucks, trailers, tents, and cranes. A huge publicity-media tent had been pitched in the parking lot. The farm plots down the knoll to the left were being mowed for post-harvest movie shots. On its own knoll to the left, the market stand pavilion glinted bright red with fake tomato plants rising above bundles of sour leaf being arranged for close-up shots.

But the smiling faces, the warm hugs, the loving welcome was the same. Aimee walked down the knoll to look out over the fields, creek, trees, and outdoor chapel. The wind was chilly, the air damp, but she felt immediate peace. This place, like no other place in her life, was where she'd felt God's purpose, God's presence.

I never felt lost here, she remembered vividly, tears suddenly blurring the beauty of the countryside. *I could always feel God's tender hand on the tiller. Every time that I felt faith wavering, God would put another great thing in our path. If we needed something, God would provide it. Our days were made up of those wonderful miracles. Every day was a miracle. Something new.*

Aimee felt suddenly overwhelmed at the bustle and noise and crowds that included cast members, movie extras, visiting media personnel, and distribution VIPs. All these people here in their small church. Their small farm. Just a short time earlier, the Spurlocks had been gathered together with Ye Win, Father Bu Christ, and others for media interviews.

"Do you remember our first meeting?" Ye Win had asked Aimee. "Before we came to All Saints that day we prayed that God would lead us to speak to the right person who would be receptive to us. You were the one who met us at the door, who told us you believe in Jesus Christ."

Yes, Aimee remembered well. How different might today have been if her answer back then had been different? *What if I'd been unwelcoming? Or made clear the last thing we needed in our church was a crowd of poverty-stricken, needy foreigners? And even before! What if I'd said no to the Holy Spirit's prompting when Michael told me he wanted to become a priest? If I'd told Michael, "Not with me you won't!"*

Then none of this would ever have come about. She would have missed being witness to God's presence moving among these very special people. *God's grace is greater than humanity. Greater than our hate. Greater than our racism. His love reaches beyond all walls and borders, beyond the color of our skin, to see only people in need of his grace and his love.*

Aimee let her gaze move lingeringly one last time across farm plots, meadow, tree line, and creek before she turned back to rejoin the noisy throng up on the knoll. Whether she ever returned here again in person, this vista, and All Saints itself, would always be to her a field of renewal. Of joy and faith and kindness. Add in, for that matter, any one of God's great mercies she'd encountered in this place.

❋ ❋ ❋

For Atticus, returning to Tennessee was returning to his childhood home, from which he'd been uprooted for his father's years of seminary, then again to move to New York City. As a small boy, he'd taken for granted the colorful multicultural church his father shepherded. The Karen children were simply his playmates, the farm a fun weekend activity. He'd ridden tractor with his father on those fields, his father's black clerical shirt and collar wilting in the heat and humidity. His dad had taught him to drive out back of the church and hadn't seemed to mind when he veered off into the deep weeds and brush bordering the fields.

Atticus remembered well his father's jubilation when he'd burst through the door to announce that God had spoken to him. But only in recent years had he learned the Karen's war-torn history or come to understand the significance of the miracles he'd been witness to at All Saints.

"I had no idea what I was getting into when we went to Smyrna," Atticus relates. "I was just happy to be back home in Tennessee. I had no idea something so incredible was going to happen to me. That I was going to get to witness God at work. It is something that I will never forget. That changed my life forever."

36

The highlight of the weekend for Michael, Aimee, Atticus, and Hadley was their return to All Saints' Sunday morning worship.

The sanctuary was crowded, smaller children sitting on parents' laps or bounced back and forth between older siblings, aunts, and grandparents to fit everyone in. Lisa Rhea's tall floor harp rippled centuries-old liturgical hymns. Filing with his family into a middle pew, Michael Spurlock was struck by the familiarity of the scene. There were Father Bu Christ and Michael Williams leading the processional down the aisle to the altar. The beaming faces of Paul and Merry Adams, Mark and Landra Orr, John and Daisy Kunoo, Christ Paw and his family, Bo Ezell and Kathy Short, Bob Druecker, and so many others.

There were changes too. Far more than the beautifully carved stone baptismal font at the rear. Some new faces Michael had met on those few trips back to Smyrna. Lisa Lehr, David and Annetta McGee, and others who'd become as committed to the mission of All Saints as the original core group.

But it was the younger generation where changes were most evident. Where were the children Michael had first welcomed to All Saints—shy, frightened by new surroundings, unable to speak a word of English? They were now teenagers, college students, even newlyweds. Their chatter as they settled into pews was not

All Saints

in Karen, but English, their clothing a mix of traditional Karen embroidery and Western styles.

But they all remembered Father Michael and swarmed around to say hello. In contrast to those early days of struggling to survive school and learn English, many were now college students or in the workforce. Father Bu Christ's oldest son, Ba Soh Wah, was now twenty-two years old, a graduate of technical college in auto mechanics, and engaged to Ciarra Black, who had once helped tutor Karen children, now a freshman in college herself. Ba Soh Wah's younger brother had just been accepted into the army. Others were studying accounting, social work, mechanics.

Another recent high school graduate, Thaw Bwe, was studying film production and had actually been hired on as an intern to the *All Saints* movie production. Other youth had gone straight from high school into the workforce at the Nissan and Tyson plants, as mechanics, administrative assistants, and more. Many were married with children of their own, the All Saints pews now overflowing with a new generation of American-born Karen.

Seeing them all took Michael back to that last week as vicar of All Saints when the flood had swept away all before it, leaving instead new, rich soil in which they had replanted seed that had given a bounteous harvest. Here in front of him was All Saints' true harvest—young men and women grown to maturity, serving God and serving their community. A future of which their adoptive country could be proud.

The adults had prospered as well. Ye Win's younger sister and her husband were two of several now working for government agencies and nonprofits that provided assistance to refugees and other immigrants. Christ Paw now worked full-time as All Saints' sexton and farm manager. If their English was still sparse, many were driving their own cars, proud owners of their own homes.

And then there was Ye Win, whose quest to provide his people with a church home had set this whole story in motion. Ye Win had already shared his own big news with the Spurlocks. Almost two decades had passed since that long-ago day, lying on a sweaty,

202

MICHAEL SPURLOCK and JEANETTE WINDLE

thin mat under the thatched roof of a refugee camp field clinic, when Ye Win had pledged to serve God with the rest of his life. He'd assumed that meant helping his own Karen people with their desperate needs. He'd carried through on his vow, speaking out for democracy in Thailand, pouring himself out to help the Karen build new lives here in America, becoming a leader to whom his people turned in crisis.

"Son, you're doing God's work," his parents had assured him. "You're being a missionary every time you see people in need and help them."

That Ye Win might one day go further, that he might be privileged to serve within God's church itself, had not been even a distant dream. Much less, that a onetime guerrilla soldier might become an ordained minister and preacher of God's Word. But now it was becoming reality, and Ye Win was following Michael's own path, continuing to serve as lay leader at All Saints while studying to complete requirements for seminary and ordination.

Ye Win's dreams and goals had grown in proportion. While remaining committed to helping Karen refugees across the United States with both spiritual and social needs, his ultimate goal is to return one day to Myanmar.

"I prayed that God would show me what he wants me to do. And God called me to become his proclaimer, his servant, his disciple," Ye Win shared fervently. "There are so many in Myanmar who need to know Jesus, and so few to tell them. And there are others who have become Christian, but they have no one to teach them the Bible, to give them solid spiritual food. Now that I have my American citizenship, I can travel back. I want to take the gospel to the villages, the jungles, the mountains of my home country. I want to find my old friends who studied with me and fought with me, and talk to them about how Christ has changed my life. That is my future dream."

Once back at All Saints, Aimee had not been slow to seek out her former choristers, and the morning service included a beautiful rendition of "Amazing Grace" in Karen and English, sung by

203

veteran and new choir members, along with Aimee's own bright soprano.

Michael and Aimee had managed to hold back tears until they were invited forward for recognition of their visit. Ye Win helped translate Father Bu Christ's personal welcome: "We came here from refugee camps, from the poorest country in the world. Father Michael was so patient with us. We are so thankful to him, and to our sister Aimee for giving so generously to our children, the choir, the women."

Six years had gone by since Michael had last stood here at this altar. Good years and trying years, for the Spurlocks and for All Saints. That the Karen still so willingly claimed Michael as one of their own was the sweetest balm to his spirit. If he never received any greater honor than to have been the vicar of this congregation, it would be enough.

As Michael stood up to address his former congregation, he spoke slowly to give Ye Win time to translate. "I love you all, and I have never forgotten you because you live in my heart. Someone asked me not long ago what I hoped people would take away from our story here at All Saints. I would hope our story proclaims that God is alive and well and very much at work in this church and in our world. As we have seen again and again here at All Saints, truth really is so much more remarkable than fiction . . . and far more wonderful."

37

*F*aith. *Community. Mission.* Three words that indeed sum up the ultimate miracle of All Saints. Faith unswerving in the midst of loss and a drawing back to faith of God's children who had lost their way. A community of different tongues and tribes and nations joined together in one family, indeed a foretaste of heaven itself. And an unwavering mission to be the hands and feet and heart and mouth of Jesus Christ to each other, to their neighbors, to a planet in desperate need of God's redemption.

"I have been asked more than once what I feel is the message of All Saints for the church across North America and even around the world," Father Randy Hoover-Dempsey says, reflecting back on his own six years in Smyrna. "All Saints was once a predominantly white, fairly wealthy church looking for its mission. Today it certainly isn't a white church. And it's not a wealthy church. Many of our members are struggling. They are dealing with psychological, physical, and financial hardships.

"But it is also a church that is working together the way a church ought to be. It is a church that has found its mission to be present in the community and help in any way God opens doors. Jesus doesn't call people just to learn biblical theology, but into community, as part of a fellowship, a family. To me, All Saints is where I've personally seen this lived out more than anywhere I've been in church. In fact, I would say that the Karen welcomed us into their family, not the other way around."

Father Randy adds fervently, "Churches sit in the midst of need, and how they respond to those needs demonstrates what it means to be a Christian. In particular, every community where there are refugees and other immigrants also has churches looking for mission. What would happen if every church currently asking what they should do next would instead say, 'We're going to welcome these people into our lives. We're going to enter into fellowship with them. We are going to fulfill our calling as the body of Christ to reach people who are strangers and aliens among us, just as we once were strangers and aliens before we received the hope of the gospel (Ephesians 2:12).'"

All Saints' current vicar, Robert Rhea, concurs passionately. "God has given us at All Saints a wonderful story of loss and redemption, hospitality and welcome, diversity and unity. Above all, a story of love's response in action. Israel was once a stranger in Egypt, and God calls us in turn to protect, honor, and care for the strangers among us. Michael Spurlock, his wife, Aimee, and the people of All Saints were open to living out the gospel by welcoming the stranger at their door. It is our prayer that God will use this story to inspire other churches and faith communities to reach out as well to the strangers, refugees, and immigrants in our midst. To welcome them with the love of Jesus."

For all his reflection, to Father Michael Spurlock, the story of All Saints remains at times a riddle. Jesus Christ so often told farming stories to convey spiritual truth. Now in the twenty-first century, the average American lives as far removed from the land as any generation in history. Their knowledge of pasturage and tillage is theoretical at best.

Yet here in the rich floodplain of All Saints' bottomland, God chose to teach his people a lesson. A lesson of death and resurrection. Quoting Saint John Chrysostom, Michael often said that a man can count the number of seeds contained in an apple, but can't count the number of apples contained in even one seed if it would just fall into the ground and die.

The world had thought Jesus dead and done as he hung on the

cross. But it was in those very moments of agony that Jesus was in truth stretching out his hands and drawing the whole world to himself that they might receive life and redemption. Just as, faced with seemingly unsurmountable losses, that small surviving group at All Saints had been able to see ahead no alternative to loss and defeat. Then God sent a beautiful group of strangers into their midst, and when they obeyed God's call to reach out in the love of Christ, resurrection came to their church.

How was it that the arrival of three strangers at a church door could so exponentially change the lives of so many people? How had Michael Spurlock been so privileged to participate in their story? The question took Michael back to those teen years and a search of which he had not then even been aware. As a young college student, his life goal had been to be a writer. Write what you know, he'd been told. And so he'd tried. If he'd failed, he could admit now it was because he'd found nothing truly worth writing about.

He'd turned then to his art, striving to capture a visual story in his paintings. Once again, the problem had not been his skill, but that he could think of no story worth capturing. So he'd set that aside.

Then he'd met Jesus Christ and found something worth his full devotion. Worth committing all his attention, his creative gifts, his strength, every ounce of his being, to communicate to others. He'd found the purpose for which he'd been searching his whole life. From that moment on, Michael Spurlock had wanted nothing more than to spend the rest of his life seeking, learning, teaching about this person and living in relationship with him.

And along the journey, God had in his own time given Michael a story worth writing. Permitted him to be part of it. To be a witness to God's redemptive grace and resurrection life. Now at last the time was ripe to put words to page.

Faith.

Community.

Mission.

All Saints.

The **Reverend Michael Spurlock** is a graduate of the University of Tennessee in Knoxville and Nashotah House Theological Seminary. He served All Saints Episcopal Church in Smyrna, Tennessee, for three years beginning in 2007. He is currently on the clergy staff at Saint Thomas Church Fifth Avenue in New York City. Michael, his wife, Aimee, and their two children live in New York City.

Award-winning author and investigative journalist **Jeanette Windle** has lived in six countries, authored nineteen books, and mentors writers on five continents. To learn more, visit her at www.jeanette windle.com.